Lying Drunk

Tony Hicks

TSPA
THE SELF PUBLISHING AGENCY

THE
SELF
PUBLISHING
AGENCY

Tony Hicks
Lying Drunk

Big Mess Press
Copyright ©2025 by Tony Hicks
First Edition

Softcover ISBN 979-8-9926832-0-2
eBook ISBN 979-8-9926832-1-9

Cover + Book Design | Angela Campbell
Editors | Stacey Roth and Chuck Barney
Publishing Management | TSPA The Self Publishing Agency, Inc.

I hate the title of this book.

Just like I hated the word "alcoholic," which I refused to use until I was in my third or fourth rehab. By then it was kind of tough to deny. I already knew, of course, but saying it out loud gave the concept legitimacy for which I wasn't ready. Anyway, I'm OK with "alcoholic" now.

Maybe the same will happen with "Lying Drunk." It's a title suggested by an industry professional for whom I have great respect. She also lives in a much nicer house than me, so ...

The biggest problem I have with "Lying Drunk" is if anyone asks my kids about the book. On one hand, that would be miraculous. It would mean I actually published a book and people are asking questions. Bad press allegedly doesn't exist (yes it does). I've already put my kids through enough. But we agreed if the title helps bring some attention to the issue and, let's face it, helps sell a few more books, then what the hell. It was the truth, and I'm pretty tired of dodging Mr. Truth.

To my daughters, mom and Bob.

Thank you for your love and faith.

Contents

Prologue

This Could Be a Lie

My name is Tony and I'm a liar … and an alcoholic.

Same thing. I'm almost positive I'm sober right now, meaning the odds of telling the truth shoot up like a rocket bucking gravity to get to the great beyond.

Sometimes you get there for a while. Then there are times, like those ancient early blooper reels of NASA's space program, in which the rocket launches, briefly soars triumphantly toward the heavens, then suddenly wobbles, skews horizontal, and explodes. It happens. It's strange. It's ugly. It's upsetting to the people watching.

But you scrape up the pieces, get a new rocket on the pad, and go again. Because what's the alternative?

Truth is a funny thing, as it depends on the person telling it. In my case, it's non-fiction, based on a true story, which may or may not be true, according to me … who doesn't have a lot of credit when it comes to personal truth. That's what happens to a guy who downed enough liquor over 30 years to kill a herd of buffalo (and probably the city of Buffalo).

People believe an alcoholic at their own risk. So should you.

A good writer named James Frey crafted a bestselling book called *A Million Little Pieces*, released in 2003. Aptly titled, it tells the story of a 23-year-old addict sent to rehab with far more detail than humanly possible. That's understandable from any author who consumed, or consumes, too many chemicals. In other words, we celebrate some of the world's greatest writers for their stories, not because we fact-checked and debated their truth to death.

A Million Little Pieces was initially hailed as Frey's autobiography and championed as genius by none other than Oprah Winfrey, the queen of celebrating humans pulling themselves up from life's smelly gutter and triumphantly remaking themselves to inspire all humanity. Oprah selected Frey's work for her book-of-the-month club, and her millions of followers rushed to buy it and all was wonderful.

Except it was the 21st Century and people had Google and someone started sniffing around and discovered Frey's book wasn't exactly 100 percent fact-driven. It was more like a "based on a true story" kind of thing. In an addicted writer's case, that should be knocked down to "based on a true story the writer thinks is true, but because he spent years burning holes in his brain with poisonous chemicals, there are some things in there that may or may not be safe to call memories."

The way Frey described his use, I promise you, means there's no way he could've remembered so many details so accurately and told a 100 percent accurate, objective story. It's just not possible (and I still look for Bigfoot near wooded areas). It's usually not possible for normal folks who don't dehydrate their brains daily. But Frey did what he could, and probably filled in some gaps.

Which is miles from saying there's no biographical story there.

But not that exact story, because the mind of a user in rehab is typically as healthy as an expired, burned egg. The mind isn't accustomed to being denied the substance it craves and gets really pissed off. It punishes its host for the absence by making them throw up, shake, suffer through aching body agony, stumble, fall down, and make their head occasionally feel like it's been attacked with a hammer. They also can hallucinate, but (trust me) not in the funny, Ozzy Osbourne taking acid and arguing with a cow kind of way.

For some, it gets as bad as seizures - which is why rehabs put so many people on anti-seizure meds. A foaming-at-the-mouth addict bouncing around a room full of already edgy patients is no fun for anyone (trust me again), especially poor nurses just trying to do their job. Anyone who knows anything about addiction knows this, or should've known.

Yet Oprah seemingly got very angry, took it personally, and went to great lengths to make her feelings known publicly. *Nobody* lied to Oprah back then. I don't believe Frey intended to lie. Perhaps technically (I realize we're getting into *Star Wars* "from a certain point of view" territory here). Frey told a story based on his truth and it took an incredible amount of guts to say what he said, so ...

Realistically, there were likely serious gaps in his memory. He probably forgot as much as he remembered, or his brain may have tried doing him favors now and again by borrowing from his imagination to fill the gaps.

Frey had to eventually appear before Judge Oprah to answer for his alleged crimes. Her indignity of supposedly being victimized by his alleged lies demonstrated she didn't get it. To be fair, non-addicts spared the horror of watching an alcoholic disintegrate before their eyes usually don't. But a man who went through even half of what Frey claimed had to answer to Oprah? She eventually apologized, but the whole ordeal just stank. This guy overcame a lot and wrote a magnetic book and Oprah made it about her.

Then again, Oprah's reaction is fairly understandable (especially when considering I'd like to write an Oprah book of the month). Which reminds me: Just kidding. Oprah was really great about the whole thing.

People don't like to be targeted by streams of lies, and people who aren't addicts don't understand how much of active addiction depends on lying. Lies are the food, water and air of addiction. It's a paradox that destroys families, relationships, friendships, and careers. Speaking of which, my overdue college loans say I'm a journalist, and journalists supposedly cling to the truth. Which was even more confusing. I was an opinionated music writer when Oprah scolded Frey, and I wrote a column defending him, saying the whole thing made me want to hug him and run right out to buy three copies of his next book. A few days later, an email from Frey landed in my inbox, saying thanks and he'd send me a copy ... or three.

I don't remember if he did. This either goes to show you alcoholics (either of us) have bad memories or we just lie too easily.

Probably both. I had someone in my life at the time who worshiped Oprah and, perhaps not uncoincidentally, reacted to my first confession of having a drinking problem by immediately making it about her. Not her fault - most people do that at first.

It's true she was victimized by my lies while I drank too much (my addiction hadn't reached life-threatening levels yet, but was well on its way). She cared only about the lying and who got blamed (me), not my health, for which I don't necessarily fault her.

The lies and broken promises are what really hurt other people, and hurt badly, because it's so personal. You love someone, they love you ... the handbook doesn't say anything about a partner drowning a relationship in alcohol and receiving that degree of lying in response.

I don't want to downsize the suffering of those living with an alcoholic. We're unpredictable, touchy, and explosively ridiculous. Without prompting, we do things like putting on a Darth Vader mask, grabbing our plastic pretend lightsaber, and running to the neighbor's house to pound on the door at 10 p.m., demanding a duel.

We unexpectedly go to work in the middle of the night and sleep in our car in the middle of the day. We also go to the hospital, throw up in public, pick fights with strangers, and generally act like loose sacks of human gasoline searching for a lit match. It's not fun for those living on the outskirts of our gravity, watching the decay.

Still, I mention Oprah and her biggest fan with whom I once lived to illustrate a point. Not to minimize lying, but to show lying is what alcoholics do. It's our most valuable way of maintaining relationships. Even when we don't have to; that's like rule one (we haven't got together to write them all out yet). Deny everything and when confronted with specifics, lie. Because we certainly don't remember all the details but need to sound like we own all the answers.

Like desperate children, we'll do anything not to get in trouble. Society throws alcoholics in jail, makes fun of us on TV, divorces us, finds us dead (in my case, alive) in a ditch, and generally relegates us to the bottom rung of the social ladder, all while telling us it's a disease and acting like it's anything but. Which is fine because cancer patients don't drive standing up around their neighborhood too fast with their head poking out of the sunroof while yelling at the top of their lungs because they, and their ten-year-old stepdaughter, thinks it's funny. I now realize she was probably laughing on the outside and terrified on the inside, now that I have enough experience with kids, and sobriety, to actually recognize things like human feelings. I've issued enough blanket apologies since I got sober that, hopefully, that incident was covered as well. Maybe I should make another call …

It's not a coincidence the first step in Alcoholics Anonymous' celebrated 12 steps is to finally have a serious grapple with the truth. You admit you're an alcoholic. That's it, and it's really a great idea. The details may or may not completely come back to you while recovering (in the spirit of truth, I never finished the 12 steps and likely never will, because I don't agree that God deserves credit for me getting sober. Let God come down here and hallucinate and blow chow on the inside of a car door and need three

11

blankets while detoxing in July. Then I'll share some credit). But I've borrowed liberally from many of those steps as I've kept trying over the years.

Of course, there were gaps in Frey's story. Of course, he didn't remember everything. Of course, he should've made it clear his book was "based" on his story. The tales with which family and friends have regaled me - and no doubt each other - about things I don't remember doing have routinely horrified me for years. As I've aged, those telling the stories have morphed into my children. Which is no fun for anyone, despite the pretend laughs.

A Million Little Pieces, by the way, is still a great book. Thanks James Frey. You gave me confidence when I decided to sit down and try to chronicle (admit) to some of this ugliness in writing.

As you're about to read - I hope - you'll see me do my best to admit when my memory might be shaky.

I've asked myself more than a few times why I'm ripping away my outer, emotional, thickened-by-self-inflicted-stupidity skin and telling 90 percent of my story. Nobody ever actually tells "all" because, even if you finally have a clear head, there are still things you still don't want to think about, let alone share. You can't.

Which is why I won't talk about prostitutes.

Just kidding … mostly.

I also know I've kept many of these stories locked up out of embarrassment and not wanting to hurt others or force them to relieve bad memories (I also really don't want to scare away any potential future ex-wives). I just want it out. It feels like a giant emotional boil that needs draining. So many years of lying require balancing the scales with truckloads of stark honesty. That just feels right, again and again. It feels clean.

It's great if it helps someone avoid the embarrassing molten hellscape of alcoholism that negatively affects everyone around the drinker. Even more importantly, if I can offer a human perspective helping people understand addicts better, then I'm happy to tell my awful stories. If I can clean my guilt and conscience with a huge power washing of truth, confronting and breaking down the untalked-about things while acknowledging the ridiculousness of alcoholic thinking, it's a win-win.

I'd also like to sell enough books to buy a KISS pinball machine.

Some things I experienced firsthand and some, unfortunately, I had to discover secondhand from other people. But I'll try telling the truth as I remember it. Unless I lie. Because I might not drink, but I'm still an alcoholic until I die.. Let's see how this goes …

Chapter 1

The Rack Card

The moment perfectly captured the steaming pile of mashed manure I'd constructed and called my life the previous few years.

Sometime in the early 2010s, I walked out of a liquor store in the East Bay Area, where I knew all the clerks by name, one still-bright weekday afternoon, big bagged bottle in hand, lacking any conscious shits to give, ready to continue my world tour of lying myopic stupidity, and abruptly threw on the brakes.

The woman in front of me already stopped to stare. She looked down and to my right.

Back at me … then down, and to my right.

To my right, by the store's front door, was a newspaper rack. I looked closer …

Oh. That's my face.

I think they were called rack cards; an advertisement sitting just below where you put coins in and pulled out the day's news-paper. For those under a certain age, newspapers were like TikTok videos, with fewer deadly health hazards and more reading.

There on the bottom half of the rack was the smiley head of an East Bay Area newspaper columnist who was feeling good about himself. Why wouldn't he? He got paid to write snarky stuff about the shallow and stupid celebrities we envy, the exaggerated antics of his own kids, and music and movies with enough confidence to spray pointed opinions around like a pop-up sprinkler dousing a golf course.

Strangers recognized him in public. He married a reader who liked his column. He judged talent competitions and won some awards. He had a weekly hour-long XM radio spot. He signed a deal with a book agent. He knew rock stars - two of whom asked him to write their books. His face was on advertisements trying to get people to subscribe to his fairly large newspaper.

He was also the guy walking out of the liquor store with a bulging, swishing paper sack at 3:30 p.m. Which, for him, wasn't unusual at all.

His (my) life was like the turkey scene in *Christmas Vacation*. It looked perfectly cooked, golden brown, juicy, and quite wonderful from the outside. But one serious poke revealed a heaving, steamy vacuum of inedible disgust.

The woman looked confused, likely wondering why the guy smiling in the ad needed two hands to carry a bottle with a handle from the liquor store to obviously day drink on a Wednesday. Two reasons: My hands frequently shook when I hadn't drank in 12 to 18 hours, so grabbing something made it less obvious. The other reason being that my hands shook, and I didn't want to drop my bottle and ruin my soon to be better afternoon.

Shaky hands are terribly inconvenient. For example, when trying to write a bad check for a 1.75 liter of vodka at 10 a.m. on a Sunday morning at Safeway, while the aging assistant manager feels so bad for you, he starts directing traffic to other lanes so you have the time to re-master this writing-your-name thing you took for granted when you were six years old.

But why the guy who was obviously mastering life was day drinking on a Wednesday afternoon was a great question I avoided like diet soda with a dead fly inside. So she looked down and kept walking. My live-and-in-person face smirked uncomfortably like I'd been caught.

Yeah. Same guy. Sorry. But … not really. Not yet. I wouldn't be sorry for years. Even though I said I was. A lot.

I wasn't sorry until I really was. They call it a bottom - the place you have to slam into, bounce around a bit like a corpse falling off a skyscraper, then vanish and burn reborn, a blazing phoenix sailing triumphantly back into real, glorious, recognizable life.

Look at that winner turned loser turned winner dominate life and fly high again! He should tell his story to groups of people desperate for inspiration. He'll become a mentor for the broken down, who want a similar return to glory, beating long odds and surviving as an example of all that's good.

Of course, people plead with him to write a book about his triumphs, documenting the bravery of digging out from his own grave and igniting an unstoppable human spirit burning eternally from the chest of this great, brave, man who will inspire millions.

No.

Still … I haven't had a drink, as of writing this sentence, in more than two years. Which once sounded impossible. So that's pretty good.

The triumph doesn't feel triumphant and probably never will. But it's way better than that place from which you keep digging your hole, clanging your metaphorical shovel against rock after deeper rock, believing that's finally the one true bottom.

They should warn people the first time they go to rehab that bottoms may vary. There's really only one true ultimate bottom, and it usually involves a casket and people standing around it, wondering if they should've done more to help. It didn't matter. The cold, quiet person in the box was going to do it until they ran out of bottoms.

Finding the bottom and taking the first few shaky steps on the road back doesn't feel good. But it beats the box or sleeping in a park in January wearing only a t-shirt and shorts. This I know.

Your "bottom" is treated as a place of legend by wise addiction veterans who have escaped. It's where you "confess" you've landed on the day you arrived at the group confessional session on the first day of rehab. And the third rehab stint a couple of years later. And the ninth in a few more years.

You feel you have to say you've hit bottom to fit in with the other addicts. It's actually a place most don't hit until death, jail, or right before a long stretch of sobriety. You always immediately tell the professionals you've hit bottom, and might even believe it. I never believed it. I was too smart, too in control. I was the guy who smirked at my bottom as I said something I thought was clever.

I didn't go to rehab after my last big bottom (as of writing this sentence). It happened when, after five days I don't really recall (I was busy), my then-19-year-old daughter stopped me one afternoon as I was on my way to the store.

I wasn't wearing pants.

"Did you need something from the store, honey?" I might have said, meaning it.

What she needed was for her father to not walk downtown in his AC/DC underwear at 6 p.m. on a Tuesday.

She brought me inside, fed me the first meal I'd had in days (I always figured frozen pizza would someday save me) and eventually convinced me to go to bed. I don't remember much from the previous five days. But I do remember thinking I finally knew I was going to die. And I was fine with it. It actually sounded like a pretty solid plan, moving forward.

I'd been sober for a year and a month, which is like seven years for normal people (think dog years). My daughter and I moved into our own apartment, which doesn't sound like an apex accomplishment of a 54-year-old man until one considers I'd lived with my 70-something mother and stepfather the previous three years, when I wasn't in rehab, one of two sober houses, jail, the psych ward, sleeping in a car, or in a park, or at the county detox.

The county non-medical (no doctors or nurses) detox ... if I can offer one piece of advice to anyone hospitalized for alcohol abuse: If given a choice between five free nights in a non-medical detox facility and falling off a 70-story building wearing a blindfold while hoping to land in a dumpster full of expired fruit ... go ahead and jump.

That's not a choice they actually give you at the hospital. So stay away from the county detox, as it's full of Salvation Army sleeper agents trying to recruit you. Which is worse than dry heaving in front of the mailman.

Just for the record, that 2021 wagon tumble was on me (they all were) as I set myself up to believe in - and bet everything on - a life that would magically appear once I was sober for a whole year. And just after I crossed my imaginary finish line, the person in whom I bet much of that motivational capital, instead of on myself, was already – and rightfully – done with my idiocy and moved on to someone else.

Months earlier, actually. But I didn't notice, as I was busy patting myself on the back and not remembering how rotten I was to her and so many others.

She saved my life by believing in me when no other adults would (who didn't give birth to me). And, no matter how things have turned out in our now non-relationship (not well), I likely wouldn't be here trying to squeeze you for 21 bucks to buy a book, if not for her. I will always love her for that alone (and maybe some other things). Life is weird and I've learned I can't say with absolute certainty that my cats won't wake up tomorrow morning wearing human clothes and dueting the Everly Brothers in fluent Swahili.

I had a choice that day and I chose wrong. For a guy who hadn't drank in 13 months, I sure remembered the way to the liquor store within a few minutes of discovering my former girlfriend's new relationship status. This was no one else's fault, especially not someone I'd seen no more than once the previous year.

I now understand why professionals call alcoholism a disease of choice. Which means you do indeed have a disease, but you have to make a really bad choice for the disease to activate, hijack your body, and try to murder you. As far as the "disease" argument, you're going to have to speak to an expert (try a drunk geneticist), but I've come to believe it. I also believe whether the disease successfully invades an addict's life is up to them and circumstances.

I made it all the way to my car before I finished my first really bad choice in 13 months and cracked that bottle. My first buzz in more than a year was honestly different – the first bad buzz I remembered. It wasn't the familiar reassurance of liquid warmth cascading down my throat, where my bloodstream would immediately and with great alacrity deliver overwhelming satisfaction to my waiting, sometimes desperate brain.

I knew the feeling of quenching the thirst of desperation. But this was different and all wrong.

From the first taste, it was dizzy and bitter, hitting me with anger and confusion. What the hell? This is how you treat me after I come crawling back? I was over it, with everyone. But there's always a feeling I can drink through whatever impediment seems to be in my way in order to feel: light, magical, and wise. The way runners or weightlifters push through hitting their imaginary wall and emerging on the other side triumphant and feeling like they did all they could.

I always drank through feeling sick, depressed, lonely, fat, dumb, ugly, tired, weak, and the effects of bad drugs. Which all drugs are at some point, whether it's during the part that's supposed to feel the best, or 12 hours later when you've run out of joy and – not uncoincidentally – drugs, and your emotions are scraping the bottom of dead-end, dirty asphalt. A drink always helps even you out and, after another and another, can even make you feel better again.

Of course, at some point you have to come down from the alcohol. Sometimes sleep works. Sometimes you just have to keep eating fast food and drinking water, then sleeping some more. Or you could do what I started doing sometime around 2011 or 2012 when it started getting really bad – just keep drinking whenever possible and do your best to keep your tank from totally emptying out. Which is obviously a mature, well-thought out strategy.

So, being sensible about this strange uncomfortable and foreign feeling of not liking the alcohol I just drank, I kept drinking. Only this occasion was different. I felt like I failed. My heart really felt broken for the first time since high school. Divorces don't count because, by the end, the magic is gone and you're just trying to salvage some feeling or standing, be it monetarily, or legally, or in the eyes of your children, or some dignity … whatever you can keep. Both my marriages lost any magic they might have had early and there just wasn't enough for the last half of each. But I didn't want divorces because I'm allergic to dramatic change and I really liked my kids -- maybe because I still behaved like one.

That was the first time I decided, at least consciously (though drunkenly), to drink myself to death.

Again, this was my decision, arriving from my twisted

imagination of a Disney happy ending I'd talked myself into. Whether she knows it or not, the person with whom I shared the make-believe future helped get me sober by giving me motivation when I badly needed it. That didn't matter, because this wasn't a joint effort. This was a relationship that existed as much in my head as in the real world by then. But it wasn't very practical, and the imagined partnership set in future love, understanding, and Jeff Buckley music certainly left out the fact I'd set multiple emotional forest fires all over the human landscape of my life, incinerating at least half the bridges I'd built with friends and family for decades. Including her. Which I guess I missed.

I somehow convinced my sick mind (they say your brain doesn't physically recover -- if it can – from alcoholism for about two years, so it was still at least half sick) that everyone would see me sober for a year and, whammo! They throw a party. Everyone hugs me, the band plays something about me being a jolly good fellow as people line up for hugs and introduce me to their children whom I forgot I met years ago, who would immediately call me Uncle Tony and invite me to their Little League games and future weddings.

Didn't happen. But at least I stopped getting emails asking what the hell I was talking about last night before never hearing from them again.

So during my five-day stupidity siesta. I stopped going to work - which I'd done the last three or four times I tumbled from the wagon. I almost got canned again, which I somehow avoided.

Staying employed is much easier, I've discovered, when not prioritizing consuming alcohol like a starving pig discovering and destroying a roadside vegetable stand.

On day six I decided to live after all, when my daughter likely saved me from a drunk-in-public arrest. I woke up the next morning, didn't drink for breakfast, and decided to endure the next four or five days of withdrawal hell with which I'd become familiar.

For those not initiated, withdrawal is only slightly worse than having violent stomach flu while trying to run a marathon in ankle-deep mud after being set on fire.

I went through it willingly. After so many false starts over three years, I was supporting myself and my daughter. I had my own place to live and a journalism job again. Best of all, I was behaving (sort of) like a dad and a responsible human again. I decided I wasn't about to give that up because of one person deciding to live her life.

I haven't drank since (at the time of this writing). I'm not exactly sure how that happened, because obviously it sure sounds like a lot of fun.

Of course, I love my kids and want to heal them from wounds I caused for years. I go to the gym every day, pretending there's still a chance I can become good looking. I stay busy and learned to love sleeping real sleep, eight hours a night, without getting up to throw up blood or urinate in a laundry basket, or finish the last bottle of the previous day at 3 a.m. while having a discussion with whatever was still alive in my fish tank.

I even, occasionally, go out to clubs and bars (with a sober friend). I go on dates with women who have a glass of wine. They ask if I mind (I have this weird streak of honesty now and always immediately warn them how I break out in idiocy when I drink). My standard reply is as long as no one brings a frosty bottle of Stoli straight from the freezer and slams it on the table before me, we're fine. And we are, especially with wine, something I only drank in the bad old days when I ran out of everything else.

I no longer drink because I can't. That's the best answer I have. If you're waiting for a magical solution to alcoholism in these pages ... that's it. That's all I got.

Not that there aren't a ton of real systemic solutions people use every day. Alcoholics Anonymous obviously has a lot going for it (sober women you can't lie to!). It's been around for nearly a century for a reason. It helped support me for years, especially when I was transitioning from rehab to real life, all 95 times I went. But finding a meeting that worked for me was difficult, because I'm not a joiner and think I'm tremendously smarter than everyone else there.

I still occasionally go to AA, but the idea of a higher power doesn't always work for me (they'd say anything could be our higher power, and I'd always think of a toaster for some reason and start laughing).

The bottom line I always tell myself is I allowed my life to become a walking nightmare that I just can't live anymore. Either I live sober or I start the process of dying all over again, something that seemingly shortens every time I drink. One of these times – if it happens again -- will be the last, whether I choose to stop or not.

I also think of my kids. They say you have to get sober for yourself but the idea of my daughters crying and needing to get away from me has kept me from diving into the smelly pool of pickled stupidity more than once.

I don't know that I'll never drink again. I hope not. But I figured I'd start writing while I still can.

These tales I tell as I remember, possibly as out of order as my life was. I tell them not necessarily for anyone else's sake, because I'm still here and not dead yet.

Chapter 2

The Stairwell: Escape from Oakland

I squeezed against the stairwell wall, trapped by my own idiocy; something I wouldn't understand for several weeks … maybe years.

Comprehension wasn't the issue; it was getting down four flights of stairs without being captured.

I'd launched, essentially, a one-man prison break.

It wasn't like alarms would go off or someone in a uniform would shoot me. The risk of being shot would actually get exponentially higher once I got to the street, if the sporadic echo of gunshots the past few weeks were an accurate gauge.

Living out there was still theory and someone else's problem. My problem was more immediate. I had somewhere to be.

CVS. Specifically, the liquor aisle.

Pressing my face against a cold concrete wall until I could smell the mildew, I hesitated. I should go back. Instead, I looked up and down and both ways (in a stairwell) and continued down another flight, advancing the commitment.

It made no sense, of course. It was late June 2017, and I'd gone nearly a month without drinking. My body was thankful. My brain was like a half-dead animal getting up and regaining its balance after lying by the road for so long, while everyone I knew drove on by.

But logic was gone. I needed out.

It was my decision-making process for years: Get a (bad) idea, start to act on it, hesitating (with good reason), then doing it anyway and briefly regretting it before doing it again.

I wore gray sweats and a *Star Wars* shirt and probably looked homeless - not the first time and certainly not the last - which would be fine once I got out. There were plenty of people in the neighborhood who resembled patched-up dirty blankets with feet.

There was a square of yellow confetti in the stairwell – the same kind, along with the blue ones that bounced around the open roof rec area when the Golden State Warriors championship parade rolled by a block away the previous week. It felt like a piece of the outside world I was missing … and probably giving up again, after this little adventure.

The fifth-floor authorities made it clear: NO LEAVING or you'll get kicked out and be sent home -- if you still had one (I had no clue) -- where everyone is tired of excuses (they were) and promises (yes) and lies (lots) and will finally give up on you (most, eventually) because you're a quitter (well …) and will probably die (almost) or end up in prison (sort of).

Institutions, jail, or death: the constant options presented if I persisted in my insanity which, in this case, was descending the stairs and exiting a 30-day urban rehab full of take-no-shit counselors, most of whom had seen and done it all.

Everyone there had to make a commitment. Mine had changed. My new commitment was stepping into that stairwell.

My blood rushed and my stomach gurgled, anticipating the warm, happy ending. No different from the times I imagined asthma clenching my lungs until liquor cleared my throat like a laser melting mid-torso mucus and dusty brain-webs.

Brain clouds, tight lungs, a cold, boredom, anxiety, shyness, writer's block, insecurity, not being good-looking enough, being challenged by my family, making simple mistakes … it all eventually vaporized into the comfortable haze of an alcoholic's self-delusion.

The catalyst was usually vodka, but I wasn't picky - bourbon, beer, mouthwash or a case of wine with a side of crushed cork briefly lodged in my throat because I couldn't get the bottle opened fast enough. I'm pretty sure I smashed the end of a bottle once after screwing up the cork (corks are serious time-killers when there are only seconds until a spouse appears). I'm sure I drank glass shards at least once. Which felt like nothing because I didn't care.

The insanity said sacrifice was necessary for the feeling of diving-into-the-pool-on-a-hot-day relief to come. Swallowing tiny glass shards that day was but a brief inconvenience on the path to getting to that alcohol. Some meth addicts allegedly crush fine glass into their powder when their nose nerves get really dull because they miss the pain. The pain says it works. I needed something to burn my throat and make me feel the outlines of my stomach. It had been weeks and I was dry as Death Valley.

The prize sat at CVS a few blocks away from that stairwell smelling like concrete faintly lined with urine. Nearly four weeks of daily showers and eating full meals had me smelling better than I had in months.

Not for long.

I was in downtown Oakland, less than a week from completing

the 30-day stay they say delivers absolution and carries you into the waiting arms of Recovery Jesus. Maybe …if you go to the right AA meetings and don't mind a big hysterical stranger wearing Wranglers and a non-ironic mustache warning you BETTER FIND GOD OR ELSE.

Did someone lose him?

That happened to me at one of those huge meetings with 200 MEN who are MEN and only allow MEN at their meetings because they have MAN things to say. Everyone is named BRO and there's a lot of pointing and hugging.

No thanks. I preferred the small meetings where we laughed and competed to see who had the weirdest story.

It was that or you go back to rehab nine or ten times – it was nine OR ten, eventually -- I'm honestly not sure. As I've alluded to, functional memory isn't an alcoholic's wheelhouse, and "alcoholic" doesn't really cover it. "Alcoholics" were old 1970s construction workers whose empty beer cans fall out of the truck when you open the passenger door.

Though in my case, it wasn't cans - it was bottles, and they exploded on my sixth-grade buddy's driveway as we dropped him off in 1979, as his parents stood there, looking like they'd been slapped with a wet fish.

My grandfather waved as we drove away. Say all you want about him not stopping to clean up the mess, but at least he was friendly.

But let's get into my weepy childhood memories later. I had

business to take care of. I had to get back to my comfort zone.

Alcohol became my food, water, oxygen, and ground on which I stood. During the previous decade or more of denial, I frequently drank from the time I woke up until I fell unconscious, sometimes multiple times a day, after which I'd just start again.

Many days, in those last couple of years, I drank at least a half gallon of vodka. I don't know -- I wasn't keeping score like in high school. I never realized how much until it was safe to hear the stories (about me, because I didn't remember much) and do the math.

So there I was, on the third floor landing in June 2017; just a few months after I offered to leave (was kicked out of) my home and angrily quit my job of 23 years a couple weeks later, the same day my dog died (seriously).

I rechecked for cameras, remembered my goal and the feeling it brought, and started jumping two steps at a time down to the second floor landing. That's where I thought I heard something echo from above (my jumping, probably).

Prying myself off the wall, I risked looking back up the center of the stairwell, like in movies right before someone wearing a sleeveless shirt shoots your face off and says something clever.

I slid back and took a big breath into my unshot face. Quiet resumed. I remember at one point thinking, if I was a rehab counselor back on the fifth floor, I'd have something rigged at the bottom, to zap escapees into running back upstairs and collapsing out of breath at my superior, sober feet.

I started looking around for tripwires, then laughed … but not too loud, in case they had the stairwell rigged for sound. I pictured the radar guy from *The Hunt for Red October* in front of his sonar screen, "Con, sonar. Russian Akula dead ahead!"

Russian vodka, more like.

My thoughts were unraveling and re-raveling. I needed a drink. I needed to go back to my room. I needed to finish rehab. I needed my family back. I needed a drink … and I needed a drink. I looked up, hesitated, and suddenly had an insane urge to cry.

I was nearly a month sober, something I hadn't been able to say for probably 30 years, at least. I felt good before today; I'd made progress. People would see – my family would see. Maybe I could go back to my wife, my kids, my job … my other dog that wasn't dead, but was 19 years old and wouldn't last long anyway.

I started welling up. Never go soft and think about your dog on a dangerous mission.

What was I *doing*? My shakes were gone. The aches were gone. No more morning dry heaves in the backyard and laying on the bathroom floor at the YMCA, trying to quietly throw up so I could theoretically exercise away the poison (it works once and suddenly you think you have this alcoholism thing beat). The daylong blackouts vanished, as had most of the lies. I was no longer stealing money from my kids, or just straight-up stealing the booze (or just drinking it in the store).

So why was I in that stairwell?

The evening's excuse was the process server who slipped

inside the locked up medical facility that afternoon.

He was an older guy with apologetic eyes. Maybe he'd once been an about-to-be-divorced alcoholic. He wasn't unexpected. Like the World War II pilots dropping leaflets en masse, urging civilians to flee before the bombs start falling, my then-wife had the decency to call my counselor a few days earlier, warning him she was about to release the big one.

I was the big one. A sweaty, bloated, pale, out-of-breath, leaky booze bomb. And she wanted to release me.

I shouldn't have blamed her, but I did anyway. I'd been trapped on one floor in a building in the middle of Oakland for weeks, trying to make things right. And if she wasn't giving me all of four weeks to change years of entrenched behavior, then I wasn't staying.

If anything, this trip was about total honesty, I told myself. And I was honestly sick of rehab and wanted to drink.

I was tired of talking about it. Every minute was about rehashing and comparing my shame with that of 30 other people. It became competitive. Who did the worst shit? Alcoholics love to gather in groups to swap stories because we can't tell normal people. It *horrifies* them.

But we laugh and say things like "I remember this time after 2 a.m. when it was either threaten a convenience store clerk with a steak knife or break into my neighbor's house to get his booze. And of course, I wasn't going to drive to the store; I'm not *irresponsible*."

Then we'd all laugh like we were insane.

I'd heard worse stories, but there's nothing worth repeating about people running a truck up a sidewalk into pedestrians. This isn't a scared-straight crowd. We were, and are, the people who think we outsmart everyone by hiding empties in the Christmas ornament tub in the garage in June, then forget until December rolls around and we're not home when the family decides to start decorating.

So consequences weren't really my concern on the staircase. I didn't really think I'd get caught, but my heart was still racing. This was the first non-controlled activity I'd had in weeks and I was probably having fun.

Right. Daring. Rebellion. Making my own rules. Nothing more American than that … I was just being me. And I was doing *great*. Not much farther …

Once I committed, things moved fast with no do-overs, like waking up in a barrel rolling violently down a hill without knowing what's at the bottom. I crawled into the barrel every day for years, giving my control to something else. Sometimes it was exhilarating, others there was embarrassment and vomit. The landing usually sucked, until I crawled back up the hill the next day.

Planning and choosing that absence of control was totally contrary and ironic. Which was one of my biggest problems.

My brain smoldered for hours after getting the divorce papers. I knew what was coming and there was no plan after that, other than a vague intent of sneaking back in and seeing what was next.

The day's redemptive work was done and the sun just set on

downtown Oakland, with a few hours until lights out. The comrades I barely knew, yet to whom I spilled my strangest secrets every day, were watching a movie, or in the rooftop rec room, or smoking without being caught.

After 25 days of rules, these three minutes in the stairwell felt liberating, as I stuck to the wall like a fake superhero, sucking up space in the narrow zones where cameras didn't reach. I knew that because, just minutes before departure, I cleverly lingered at the nurse's station, making small talk while slipping behind the counter to see the camera feeds from the lobby and stairwell until I had an idea of my escape route.

I was a fucking superhuman, totally clever, definitely-smart-er-than-them, alcoholic *commando.*

As far as I was concerned, the slate was clean, the liver was robust, and the brain craved adventure (actually, the brain was just starting to process another divorce and was terrified of the future as a 50-plus-year-old man with no career, no money, and no more access to a bed at his mom's house).

I guess my plan was to continue the last few nights of my stay, only drunk. How could that not work in a place full of sober drunks and people medically trained to detect drunks when they see them?

I was essentially giving up on myself and finishing rehab. Or maybe not. I was in pain. But I was still alive for a reason: I was really good at being an alcoholic.

More stairs; No humans in the lobby, or the hallway on the other side. With cameras pointed toward the walking space, I slowly crept around the perimeter to the stairwell door, like I was on the outer ledge of a skyscraper. Unlocked.

I thought I heard the theme from *Mission Impossible* in my bent brain, which made me smile.

No *smiling*. I'll smile when I get back and feel *great*. Being sober in rehab, which of course is the point, still sucks.

I knew they locked the entire building where it meets the sidewalk at some point, but panic bars on the doors to the street would get me out. Getting back in could be problematic.

I'd blow up that bridge when I crashed into it.

I hit the bottom landing, shoved the door, and made sure the knob on the other side wasn't locked. I tiptoed into the lobby, probably looking like an escaped lunatic (technically, kind of true). I extended my head around the corner like a nervous kid playing spy.

No security guard. Perfect. I could see the street beyond. I ran, mouthing "shitshitshitshtshitshit" through clenched teeth like I was about to Butch Cassidy off a cliff. I wedged a pen into the doorframe, in case the guard came back (I still don't know if there was a guard, but I humored myself).

Freedom!

Looking left and right - because that never looks suspicious - I rounded the corner and started running the two blocks to CVS.

What a sight: A desperate middle-aged suburban caucasian addict dressed in a cheap blue *Star Wars* shirt and sweats, running through downtown Oakland on a Friday night.

My leg started cramping when I literally hit the door, threw on the brakes, ignored the people looking at me, made a couple of turns into the liquor aisle, and stopped.

I still had a choice. Twenty-five days of honesty felt like an absolute miracle to someone who no longer believed in miracles. The longest I'd gone without alcohol the previous decade was six days when my doctor told me I had diabetes (which has since, always, pretty much and very mysteriously vanished once I stopped drinking, along with my former high blood pressure problem).

I was doing so well, which meant I was starting fresh. Screw it. I already escaped. If caught, they'd probably throw me out even if I didn't drink. By then it was found money; I'd be stupid not to.

I grabbed a bottle of red Smirnoff. "Come on," I whispered, like I was sneaking my high school girlfriend out her bedroom window.

I acted cool at the checkout, in case someone recognized me as an escapee from the nearby booze jail. On Saturdays, counselors escorted us on neighborhood field trips to buy acceptable products to take back to the unit. Because they didn't let us have caffeine, I usually spent my CVS time stuffing my pants with caffeine pills. Just because I was sober didn't mean I wasn't still acting drunk.

I calmly made my purchase, said thank you, and speedwalked my way to the door. I mentally brushed off the slice of fear that was dripping into my brain. I had it! I ran back to the building, peeked comically around the corner again, then retreated a few steps and - catching my breath - cracked the bottle, like my first present Christmas morning.

Remember *The Wizard of Oz,* when everything goes from black and white to lovely warm color? It was like kissing the person you love most after not seeing them for months. It was like jumping in a pool after hours of driving Highway 5 down California's barren Central Valley in August with no AC.

I felt invincible. Yes, I was going to march back into that building and commence learning about getting sober. I'm a GODDAMN HERO.

I only finished half the bottle. I didn't need more - my tolerance was low. I hid the rest in a bush – which turned out to be a strategic blunder. Back through the lobby and up the stairs and to the fifth floor I went, without fear (I fearlessly tripped and fell only once). I went up to the roof and sat down next to Michael at a picnic table. After about 15 seconds, I noticed he was looking at me and smiling.

"Did you sneak out and get something?"

Shit.

That was fast and wasn't supposed to happen. So like a drunk moron - which I was - and not without pride, I confessed. Michael was some sort of bright military scientist who also was good looking. He'd been thrown out of this place a year earlier because one of the two women in the program with whom he was making sweet rehab love found out about the other and set off a screaming truth bomb that got them all ejected. I think the facility had a military contract that greased Michael's return.

Michael talked well, in a unit full of incredibly vulnerable people. Some might call him a predator; my twisted up, barely-hydrated brain saw a cool guy. He and I snuck real coffee into the unit whenever they let us out for a nearby outside AA meeting. The meetings are easy to find because every third building in Oakland belongs to Kaiser Health.

But even half-pissed, I knew my face was glowing like the sun and I was sweating like a tweaker on a treadmill, despite sitting outdoors at night. So after swearing a completely untrustworthy addict to secrecy, I excused myself and went to bed. My roommate was 200 years old and unconscious.

I made it through the next day, remembering my bottle was still outside, waiting in a bush. I did *Mission Impossible 2: An Even Worse Decision* that night and finished the bottle. Which wasn't enough -- because that's how this thing works. However, you were drinking at your worst is how you're drinking within one to three days of relapsing. No one believes it until it happens to them five or six times. I didn't ... but I do now, which is why I'm alive.

It wasn't enough. I went back to CVS ... once, I think. I'm not sure. I got a five-hour day pass the next day, Sunday, to spend with my eldest daughter. I couldn't drink around her, so the withdrawals were already back by mid-afternoon. They breathalyze inmates upon completing their visit. I failed, of course. All I remember after that is, at one point, having a bottle to tuck under a mattress. So I may have snuck out again (don't ever hide alcohol under a mattress, even if you think it's genius).

I woke up the next morning feeling like I'd been clubbed. I was in a room I didn't recognize, alone. I stood, failed at trying to make myself look presentable, and walked out into the hallway. They'd put me next to the nurse's station, which was the detox wing. I wasn't detoxing yet. I was in a netherworld between really drunk and seriously confused.

I straightened up, walked past the overnight nurse who wasn't paying attention, and went back to my room, where my mattress was left hanging off the box spring, like the police just tossed a suspect's house. Embarrassed, I quickly packed and went to the nurse's station and said I was leaving. I only did that to get my phone back (which they take when you arrive) so I could call an Uber.

This time I took the elevator.

Chapter 3

The Storm Before the Storm

So I was out. Yay.

Now what?

I felt like William Wallace screaming "FREEDOM" as the British disemboweled him. Which was kind of the same thing, except it was my innards and my disembowelment was taking much longer. Now I was walking back into the town square and re-strapping myself to the torture table.

I'd wiped out nearly a month of good work.

I've learned through online dating you have to call any kind of therapy/rehabilitation/crying in front of strangers "work" because adult women smarter than men want mates who "work on their shit."

Which sounds a bit counterproductive, because they seem to require prospective partners to have lots of issues in the first place, so we can then pay someone to "work" on them. But you can read about that in my next book, "How to Pay Dating Sites Thousands of Dollars To Never Get a Girlfriend."

For now, back to my dilemma on an overcast July morning in 2017. What the hell does someone do when they've escaped rehab and no one knows?

You might say: "So what? It was only 25 days." But that was more than four times as long as I'd been sober the previous decade. Six days, at the time, seemed like an award-winning accomplishment.

Indeed, the bright side was I didn't drink for 25 days. Which I considered wiping the whiteboard clean so I could start filling it up again with awful shit that would embarrass me to the point of writing a book someday.

The bad news was I was now behaving like a rampaging, very drunk and hungry, chimpanzee.

So much for my plan to sober up, work on getting my family back, and somehow get my career back. None of that even crossed my mind the previous few days, or the next week or two.

I'd talked my sister into ditching her house sitter before I left rehab to let me watch her place while she and my nieces were out of town. Right … me alone fresh out of rehab, but not even close to rehabilitated, isolating in a nice house in a quiet neighborhood. Excellent plan - almost as good as when I left rehab a year later and moved straight to downtown Vallejo, with a frequent audio backdrop of gunshots and a liquor store literally right behind my new home. And on the next block. And on the next block … which was helpful, because not all liquor stores open at the same time every morning.

Predictably, I was hauled away by paramedics and hospitalized within a couple weeks of launching my Vallejo adventure. Then the lady landlord whose name I don't remember (but do remember her admitting she was decades behind on taxes and was afraid the Feds would come get her at night) kicked me out, she said, because she kept hearing crashing and yelling from my room in the middle of the night.

Which was mysterious to me because, outside of blacking out, falling over my night table and shredding my rotator cuff, I don't remember anyone else being there.

When I was bugging out of rehab in Oakland, I returned to CVS for a morning bracer and walked to the MacArthur BART station and hopped a train to Lafayette, where my sister lived.

My poor sister. Her 2017 was much worse than mine, and the last thing she needed was her selfish, out-of-control alcoholic brother making things worse. So I did, as I'd slurped away all empathy and common sense months earlier.

No, it doesn't make any sense. None of it does. Lying is standard, self-preservation feels tied to availability of your substance, and the future isn't the future. It's getting your next dose of whatever.

Just before I parted ways with my life after the 2016 holidays, I took a photo of that year's Christmas tree tilting at a 45-degree angle, like a cruise missile about to launch from a battleship, which I'm sure looked fine at the time. My sister was going through a life and death situation, which is her story to tell. I'll just say her year was bad and I was so dug into the bottle, I was of absolutely no help to her or anyone else. I was a selfish bastard of an alcoholic who couldn't even see over my pile of self-induced misery.

But no one could say I didn't get the Christmas tree up and ready to launch, in case we were ever attacked by neighbors.

I don't remember much of the week at my sister's, other than briefly trying something from under the bathroom sink that smelled like alcohol, when I couldn't get to the store (Uber gets really complicated when you forget where you are or how to use a phone). It was either mouthwash, cologne or … I honestly don't know. Maybe there was a reason my pipes felt so clean the following month.

I finally figured out the pesky phone and called my mom so she and my stepdad Bob -- with whom I'd lived for a few months before rehab – took me back in. They'd evict later. Then take me back in. Then evict me and … I lost count. To be fair, it happened a lot, and my math skills weren't at their peak. Like I said, I honestly also lost count of how many times I officially enrolled in rehab those years.

When Mom and Bob came and got me, it reminded me of the time she had to pick me up from school in ninth grade because two friends and I thought it would be fun to put our faces in my parents' liquor cabinet for lunch. She wasn't happy either time though, unlike ninth grade, I didn't pass out sitting straight up when getting the lecture.

So I went back with my family and pretended to be sober while plotting to somehow put my own family back together. It's safe to say I was missing the point. Especially once I figured out I still had that spy-on-your-loved-ones app (or whatever it was called) on my phone.

My estranged wife spent a lot of time the previous few months with a co-worker and "friend" with whom we used to party quite a bit. Of course, he drank as much as me, which actually isn't for me to say (but he did). Irony can be pretty ironic. She -- his boss or former boss -- used to suspect him of drinking at work, she'd tell me. But she didn't fire him, which I guess shows how bad I was. And how good of "friends" they were.

Yes, I was an alcoholic whose wife wanted him to quit for years … until it was time to throw a party. Birthdays, Fourth of July, Halloween … Thursdays, whatever. Then I guess I wasn't an alcoholic anymore, because there was a lot of booze at my house. And I know I didn't buy it all, because it wasn't hidden in the garage inside a tub marked "camping gear."

To be fair, booze was always considered "camping gear" with my group of friends.

I'd married two women with the same name (not at the same time). Like the first one, the second wife had a daughter around elementary school age when we met. Like the first wife, the second one - code named X2 - gave birth to another daughter with me. I was with both wives of the same name about 10 years. We're all Leos. I don't believe in astrology, but it's still weird (the next woman for whom I fell is also a Leo. I don't do math as a rule, so you figure it out).

I was with X2 when the day-drinking really took off. I could have been married to Salma Hayek pleading with me to stop and still would've drank more than the floodgates on the Hoover Dam.. My arrogance had grown; I had a job in which people occasionally recognized me or my name in public. I got some attention for a few years, which is how I met X2. I was hired to write a book that fell through. A literary agent approached me about another book. Two famous musicians asked me to write their autobiographies (I screwed up one offer and the other guy died which, I guess, meant I was fired).

My drinking increased with my confidence during my second marriage. At some point, I agreed again to attend outpatient rehab, basically - in my mind - to cure me of day drinking. My clever, meticulously-planned strategy was to only drink when the sun was down or on the way home from rehab. I believe I went to rehab outpatient rehab three times during our marriage.

On X2's birthday in 2017, after we split, I checked in with my 9-year-old daughter - who we'll call Lucy (because that's her name). Mom wasn't home; she was at a "work thing." Her older sister was watching her. So, out of curiosity (drunkenness) I looked up her mom's location on the phone app thing that people think is a great idea until you find out your former significant other is doing other significant things with another man.

That's weird, I thought. She's having a work event at a bed and breakfast around Carmel.

That evening didn't go well.

In the following months, her "friend" I'd come to think of as "Shitbag" (SB) helped her pack up my stuff - in boxes with his name on the shipping labels, because I wasn't already insulted enough. He moved into my room, bed, and probably used my night table, which somehow bothered me more than anything else.

They also replaced my then 15-year-old daughter with his kid and mine got shipped to her mother in Placerville, then eventually across the street from the Scientology center in Clearwater, Florida.

I was so out of it, I allowed her mother to take her to Florida in the middle of high school because my first ex-wife, code named X1, was allegedly getting a reality show because she was a psychic. Which I really wish I was making up but, on the other hand, was totally par for the course in my bizarro-year of 2017.

The last time I interacted with SB before confirming his new status around my house was a couple days before X2''s birthday. Fascinatingly enough, I was meeting the girl for whom I was about to fall for (and had secretly admired for years). I showed up to our first lunch date - which was honestly as friends (at the time) - and SB was actually sitting two tables away.

As an aside, it's almost funny how I've thought of him as SB for years. In 2023, after two years of sobriety, I finally committed to taking my younger daughter full time, after SB decided my daughter didn't clean up the excretion of his dogs in the backyard fast enough, and made good on his longtime threat to put a bag of dog shit in her bed.

Right. Shitbag crossed the line with a shitbag.

But back in 2017, when I was trying to stare at the lovely woman with whom I was about to dine, I was intercepted by SB and a fake bro hug. He'd likely been sleeping with my (estranged) wife for months and he gives me a bro hug. Maybe it was his way of thanking me for helping him get a girlfriend.

I suspected he was already much closer with my wife than I'd been for a long time. But I didn't know for sure, and there was a funny, smart and beautiful woman waiting at the next table. So I skipped the confrontation. I'd try to ignite that confrontation later after verifying his new status and, to be totally honest, am very glad I couldn't find him, because my alcohol-fueled secret plan didn't involve inviting him to a bro hug and lunch.

The woman at the table was worth every minute we spent together the next few years, even if I regret causing her so much pain and trouble. She became a big reason I kept trying, at least, to get sober. I did get sober, but probably too late, as she got tired of me drinking too much and acting like a befuddled baboon. Our stories, some absolutely beautiful and some pretty horrifying (on my end, mostly), remain between us -- at least on my end -- for whatever that's still worth.

Nevertheless, I spent the next two or three years trying to straighten up, drinking, apologizing, apologizing some more, etc. (alcoholic readers and their co-dependents are nodding their heads at the time-killing cycle of brazen stupidity). What could've been a great relationship ended up breaking my stupid, pickled heart because I couldn't get it together.

But shortly after I confirmed my still-legal-wife was sleeping with SB, I ramped up the drinking and vacationed at the hospital for my 50th birthday. Just before midnight, my 70-year-old mother found me unconscious in a car (mine, hers, a neighbor's ... still not sure) and somehow got all 215 vodka-soaked pounds of unconscious me to the hospital, where they found seven times the legal limit of alcohol in my blood, more alcohol than what killed Led Zeppelin drummer John Bonham.

On the bright side, as a drummer, I finally found something I could do better than John Bonham.

I discovered my .56 blood alcohol level a bit later when my in-patient rehab counselor looked up my medical history and, still staring at the screen, said "This CAN'T be right." It was like watching Han Solo not grasping the Death Star wasn't just some moon.

That episode sent me to Scotts Valley in the beautiful Santa Cruz Mountains, at a rehab in a redwood forest called The Camp, where I was almost the oldest guy there. Being in rehab with a bunch of 20-somethings wasn't the place for me, but the trees were nice and I didn't escape.

Though maybe I should've, especially the night one of my cabinmates – a 19-year-old wannabe gangbanger whose rich dad sent him there as punishment for wrecking his BMW or something – dropped his drawers and launched himself at me when I was falling asleep. He wagged his noodle in my face and screamed to the laughter of the other inmates.

He put it back pretty fast once I started swinging. The other idiots got between us and Mr. Dickshake got kicked out a few days later after I shared that funny little tale with management.

I'm not typically a snitch. But, at the time, I was very serious about straightening myself out. And very grumpy for putting myself in such a position. Plus I typically don't like other men's junk in my face, especially when they act like I used to act when I was his age.

Those annoying 20-somethings with their wide-open futures,

and the forced sobriety, and the losing-my-wife-and-family stuff while I was 90 miles away didn't put me in the best mood that month. In terms of the 12 steps, I was probably on negative six.

The next nine months I stayed at the parents' house, failing to get jobs and mostly ignoring my kids because I was ashamed (and drunk), and chasing a woman who was still technically not available. I prepared for the holiday season by spending six December days in the hospital. That was the first detox during which I hallucinated, or so I was told. I was apparently having discussions with mice standing on my hospital room TV.

Oh - like you wouldn't answer if a mouse stood up on your TV and started talking to you.

My motor skills deteriorated enough, even after a week of sobriety, I couldn't walk without help when I got home. At least one doctor said I might've had a small stroke and gave me a walker, which I used for a couple days, up until Christmas Eve, when my kids were coming over. I wasn't drinking again (yet) but still qualified as an absolute disaster and I wasn't going to spend Christmas with my kids and a walker, like some crippled old bastard.

I mean - I WAS a crippled old bastard, at least for a while. But that didn't mean my kids had to know. They were already worried it was going to be my last Christmas.

I was back in Oakland by June 2018, starting my third stay at a go-away rehab in a year and making new friends. The first few days are always spent detoxing. The first time I experienced detox was during a lull in my first post-marriage drinking rampage of 2006.

I've already mentioned it, but it merits more discussion for those thinking about taking up the glamorous life of a serious alcoholic.

Detox is your addicted body screaming like a naked, teething baby ripped from a warm blanket and tossed into a wet snowbank. It's having history's worst case of flu in an ant-infested Arizona motel room in July with no air conditioning, window shades, or cold water. Except with more exciting dry heaving, confidence-building soiling yourself, and begging a God you may not believe in to kill you.

Detoxing in rehab is better, though it still sucks. But at least they have piles of drugs and mostly leave you alone to sleep and/or look at the wall and talk to bugs for three to five days. Except at the rehab attached to the stairwell, which usually forced you to go to group sessions while still detoxing. But you had an excuse in case you dozed off or threw up, or both (it happened).

They once made a poor woman, whose name I can't remember, sit through a session when she clearly didn't feel well. She was in her 40s and didn't look a minute younger than 75, the actually-rare stereotypical, homeless-looking crack addict character type from a bad 90s movie who usually doesn't end up in a clean rehab that takes insurance. She'd talked a lot of mostly incomprehensible, confrontational babble the four or five days she'd been there, and it was known among the inmates she'd been orally performing on a 18-year-old patient in a bathroom the previous day.

So no one knew how serious it was when her seizure started (Seizures can be a component of serious withdrawal and can be fatal). But there wasn't much doubt once she was foaming at the mouth, hitting her head on the table, then gagging and collapsing to the floor. The nurses worked on her until the paramedics took her away. A few days later, there were competing stories as to whether she died or fell into a coma. But she was gone.

She didn't take the stairs. Nor did I this time. It was getting to be routine. But at least I was a bit more serious. More confetti rained as the Warriors won another championship in 2018 and had a parade a few blocks away from where I was stuck in rehab again.

One of the great mindfucks of addiction is how falling so low inflates your ego so high, at least at first. It's the self-delusion about always being the smartest person in the room, because your behavior wouldn't have lasted so many years without developing some serious cleverness. At least as far as you're concerned.

It's also hard work being an addict, because you think you're inventing new ways of outsmarting spouses, wives, parents, friends, bosses … anyone who might have a negative reaction to you needing to dump down a water glass of vodka before even considering a semi-useful conversation.

Then you get to rehab, everybody starts swapping stories, and you wonder how all these people stole your great ideas.

This wasn't one of those rehabs they advertise on late-night TV, with calm, slow-moving people smiling through soothing group hikes overlooking the gentle green slopes of the Napa Valley. Just getting away from their addiction by replacing it with calm reassurance that everything is going to be *fine*. We *care*, and we're here to *listen*.

That works for some people, but I was way past hiking. I was instead confined to an old hospital, staffed by former addicts who laughed when you lied to them, because they know all addicts are liars, and don't hesitate to say so. It was a place where you heard gunshots outside at night, down the block from a part of town that later burned during riots. There were no nature walks and suntans here.

That doesn't make me tougher than the average alcoholic, perhaps weaker and just more screwed up. I was years past getting to choose a vacation rehab. I was a mess and still didn't really care.

Which really only meant I was there to straighten up the old mess to make way for new messes. It was always about cleaning up enough to restart from scratch, a concept fueling my behavior since the first time I went to rehab 12 years earlier.

This time, I thought I was trying to save a relationship we hadn't fully built. The previous time it was to save a marriage. The first time, way back in 2006, was to save a first marriage because I had a four-year-old and just bought a big house. I'd finally progressed to the point of drinking until the only way to recover was to go to the emergency room. You're fucked once the folks in the ER start to get to know you, and just stick you in the hall on a gurney for six or eight hours. Another helpful tip for aspiring alcoholics: You'll get no sympathy at the hospital or from the paramedics who take you there. One paramedic once told me I was "just a fucking drunk."

I mean … he was right, but that was kind of rude.

So I talked my way back into the same Oakland rehab from which I escaped the previous year, and actually made it through 30 days ... before getting the bright idea to move to Vallejo, a city on the northern edge of the bay with some rough spots. One of which I somehow found.

I'd already been in some outpatient programs for various reasons over the years -- to control day drinking, to say I was trying to quit, to save a relationship that was already dead ... whatever. Many of the outpatient counselors were younger than me and their knowledge of addiction came from studying. Many of them were good at their jobs. But the best example of why that didn't always work was the counselor who authoritatively told the group caffeine addiction is just as bad as "crack cocaine." The laughter couldn't be helped..

Of course, you don't correct them. You say "I've finally hit rock bottom (you haven't) and I have a problem I want to solve (you don't) ... my name is Tony, and I'm an alka (mutters something sort of sounding like "holic," though it might as well be "seltzer" for all my non-sincerity).

Yaay .. you did it! Step one, only 11 more to go! I'd pretend to be moved, watch a few people cry, hug a stranger or two. Then I'd stop by the store on my way home to grab a bottle of vodka to ingest in the car before passing out an hour later at home.

But, of course, you don't say their college degrees have less value than being a former homeless addict. I believe in college. Some of those counselors do their job well and they all try. But to rehabilitate hopeless addicts, college is probably only useful as a supplement to really understanding how, for example, it feels to wake up on someone's lawn in Carson City without knowing how you got there (because it was on my way back from the whorehouse … duh).

You do what you're told because maybe this time, once you "graduate," you can take your certificate home and say "See, it says right there I'm cured. Now you can't divorce me."

Then they do anyway. And you know you deserve it.

By the time you're on a stairwell, trying to escape people trying to help you, you no longer have a choice. At least it feels that way. There's no time for more pondering how such a seemingly bright brain ends up on the ass end of so many rotten decisions.

Gradually, over the years, drinking became survival. If I got a cold, an asthma attack, couldn't sleep, had a hangnail, didn't like what was on TV, drinking solved the problem. It became the air I needed to survive.

Thirty years before the stairwell, I almost died from asthma, until the paramedics showed up and shot me full of adrenaline as my body was shutting down. You know your body is shutting down because things start … evacuating. Which also happens sometimes when you're detoxing from alcohol withdrawal (in my case, while driving to the liquor store because detoxing had become pretty inconvenient).

Even with heavy pants, getting that first buzzing burst of alcohol felt just like the adrenaline needle - safe and warm like a full body blanket on a cold night or sun cutting through overcast. Everything was possible again (once I changed my pants).

By the summer of 2017, alcohol filled my soul in ways humans just couldn't anymore. I certainly couldn't.

Chapter 4

Pulled Over in Bed

I just settled in to sleep one night, probably in 2009 or 2010, when something woke me up.

I'm guessing now it was probably the two cops standing at the end of my bed.

It actually wasn't the first time I had police officers show up where I was sleeping. When my friends and I were a week away from graduating high school, we (my friends, me, our pony keg) went to Santa Cruz to spend the night on the beach.

It was just like in the movies. Guys and girls around a campfire, the sound of crashing waves and the dim white foam rolling back and forth where ocean meets land, the laughter, people occasionally sneaking off in the dark to do things people do in the dark on a beach. At one point, we noticed we were running out of firewood and needed to go gather more from the forest.

The problem was there was no forest; only a path leading up to some beachside homes, with wooden steps, wooden handrails, and wooden planter boxes on wooden decks (which we ignored because we were drunk, but not stupid … well, not *that* stupid). And, as far as we remembered, wood burns.

It wasn't long until three or four of us were double-timing it down the beach, like drunken Marines (sans weapons, thank God), carrying a couple long wooden rails over our shoulders. And, obviously to keep everyone alive and not freezing to death in California's calamitous June weather, we broke up the wood, and spent the next few hours gleefully burning it to stay alive.

That turned out to be a mistake.

Inside a tent is where I woke up the next morning, as someone opened the flap and said loudly, near my feet, "All right, everybody UP."

It was a sworn officer of the law. At the end of my sleeping bag.

When we all managed to roll outside, there was another cop and three older men standing around the smoldering ruins of last night's camp fire. They were muttering to each other and pointing, as if identifying which piece of wood was from whose property. There was apparently a lot more than I remembered grabbing the night before.

So a few of us got arrested - not the girls because, though drinking some, they seemed -- as usual -- to have a much better grasp on the idea of cause-and-effect than three cars full of teen boys. True, they were profiling us as they went straight for the guiltiest-looking boys, which happened to be 100 percent accurate.

We didn't get cuffed, but gave them our information and signed promises to appear, which we did three months later. We had to pay for the fences and got six months of juvenile probation, as I was 17 at the time of the crime. Some of the others were 18. We were all young. And stupid.

I actually had a probation officer for six months. Which made me feel like I had some new (suburban) street cred, even though I only saw my probation officer once in his cubicle in an office park. He looked about as excited about my ongoing rehabilitation to re-enter society as a bus driver staring at a sandwich.

After paying my debt to society, the police again showed up at the end of my bed a couple years later, in a hotel room. It was an age - 19 or 20 - when all you needed was some drugs and a hotel room with a few friends and you had something incredibly important to do for 15 hours, depending on which drugs you brought.

We had meth, which was the lubricant of so many world-altering plans, superbands formed, incredible (no) songs written, and generally important communication with others by everyone talking at once, making a sound like a dozen decks of cards shuffling non-stop for hours, sincerely believing you were changing each other's lives.

No, I definitely wasn't asleep that time.

My friends and I entered the dead zone around 2 a.m. – where we were almost talked out because of the speed. We called it crank, people now call it meth … whatever the name, it's usually made by combining a bunch of chemicals sold in bottles with skulls and crossbones on the side.

I remember some pockets of the room were still blabbing away. I was on the bed, watching *Kelly's Heroes*, thinking in my drug-induced brain hysteria - "My God, this is the greatest movie ever made because, TELLY SAVALAS IS A GODDAMN GENIUS OF AN ACTOR …" and so on.

I heard a creak and saw a German shepherd walk into the room, at the end of the bed I was on. Which I thought was a bit strange.

Then I saw the cops at the other end of the leash. Which just ruined everyone's fun.

Seeing police walk into your hotel room unannounced when

you're wired on crank is about the only thing that can make your body feel even more shocked than actually doing the drugs themselves. We all froze.

Like us, the dog apparently had a nose for drugs. Only he didn't actually snort them, as far as I knew. But he could smell them from outside a closed hotel room door, when the police were on our floor breaking up a party at the other end. The police said Mr. Furry Fantastic Nose stopped outside our door and explained to his handlers there were some 20-somethings on the other side talking like machine guns, forming their next band, and saying how much they loved each other while repeatedly organizing tiny bars of soap in the bathroom.

Robo-dog went straight for an old Adidas bag on the floor that, suspiciously, looked like something I'd been carrying around since ninth grade. The police, who were terribly calm for being around a roomful of freaked-out young men with long hair on drugs, sauntered over to the bag and asked if they could take a look. Someone finally nodded, as we were way too scared to remember how to speak.

They pulled out a large bag of white powder, a scale, and some smaller baggies, for dividing up the goodies (now baddies). They asked who the bag belonged to. No one said anything, so I quickly remembered the one phrase that always, without fail, gets young people off the hook with the authorities:

"It's not ours," I cleverly volunteered.

To their credit, the cops didn't fall over laughing or shoot me for being stupid. As one sort of nodded, the other reached into the bag and pulled out a wallet, reached inside the wallet, and pulled out a California driver's license.

Huh … that picture looked a lot like me.

"This your license?" the police officer asked, somewhat rhetorically.

"Well … yeah," I said.

"So is this your bag," he asked.

I sensed where this was going. But I was ready to outsmart this guy.

"Yeah … but the stuff inside isn't mine."

He looked at me, so I went ahead and closed the circle of stupidity. I really said it:

"It belongs to a guy who was here earlier."

"OK," said the officer. They asked us all to sit on the side of the bed, while they checked everyone's IDs (and, I'm sure, everyone's wallets for more drugs). One officer asked us "Any razor blades inside any of these?" "No. no … no sir," we said, lying. Well, at least one of us was lying, but probably forgot. It didn't matter - if they found one, they didn't say.

The cops conversed. I was looking at the handsome dog and, being of sound mind and all that, decided I should pet the good boy. Before I could reach, one of the cops said "Don't even think about petting him."

But he looked so friendly …

A few seconds -- or years, I couldn't be sure -- later, one of the officers pointed at me. I'd been thinking I was screwed, of course. As I was mentally rehearsing my one phone call from jail, the cop asked me to get up. I did, and turned around with my hands behind my back, so he could handcuff me.

"What are you doing?" he asked. Then he laughed, "No no no, come here. Pick up that bag and follow me."

So, absolutely perplexed, I picked up the bag of white powder and followed him into the bathroom, wondering if he was going to take my drugs and wrap some soap in a towel to beat me to death. He pointed to the toilet. "Put it in."

Shocked, I dropped the entire bag in the toilet like it was on fire. He started laughing again. "No, pick up the bag and dump it out."

WhatsthatagainSir??!!

"Dump it out."

So I did, then ripped up the bag and flushed it too, at his request. He told me to go back and sit down with my friends.

"Look, we're not going to lecture you about this stuff, because we know you know better," the officer with the leash of the handsome death beast in his hand told us. "You got lucky tonight, because it was us. Now get your stuff and get the hell out of here. Right now."

We got lucky because we were dumb suburban white boys and, I imagine, because they didn't have a warrant or it was the end of their shift or something. Thankfully, it was the first time that night I opted not to talk. Maybe we really were just lucky to get a couple of cool cops. Anyway, we gathered our things and, as the cops left, just about started crying. All of us. We escaped.

It was my first major dodge. I would keep dodging them way too long, until I didn't. Thankfully I didn't kill anyone, or myself, along the way. But it wasn't for lack of trying.

Until I didn't, I had a long history of dodging bullets like Samuel Jackson's Jules in *Pulp Fiction*.

A year after watching a guy get busted for selling a large quantity of pot that I financed (he didn't talk and I didn't ask for my money back), on my 23rd birthday, I talked my way out of a DUI … with five other guys in my car with open containers, one of whom will remain nameless (Sal Gallagher) deciding to pop off to the cop about not having probable cause.

The cop just looked at me and said "I see you brought your lawyer with you tonight. Get out of the car." Having a lawyer wouldn't have been the worst idea: We had 300 pounds of stolen dirt in my trunk. We'd decided our friend Bob - who had to drive to LA early the next morning in his bloodthirsty quest to get a record deal – needed a beautiful garden planted in the back of his truck for drivers to admire on southbound Interstate Highway 5.

Many years later, Bob was the Bob Reid who went viral on social media - "Who's Bobby Reid?" -- for having a *Fear the Walking Dead* episode dedicated to him (he was a crew member), after he died in 2019 after falling asleep at the wheel one night. Bob was another high school buddy, a musician to whom I looked up and with whom I did stupid things that frequently involved alcohol, though I don't think alcohol played a part in his death.

Once Bob and I and another buddy, who now masquerades as a responsible Disney executive, were confronted by police while carrying a beer bong and crossing the street on our way to a party. The officer asked why we had a funnel connected to a long plastic hose.

Bob quickly placed the funnel on his head and said we were going to drama rehearsal. We were performing *The Wizard of Oz*, he explained. And he was playing the tin man.

The cops laughed and let us go. Just like in 1990, once I promised the Dublin police officer I'd drive straight home and never again go anywhere with those mouthy young men in my car, who I barely knew and certainly didn't like, and the policeman let us go.

When we left, we were smart enough not to break into the same fenced-in garden store again, and went and stole our (Bob's) plants in a different city. I don't think Bob appreciated the time and care we put into it (though he got even with me about 18 months later in a particularly brilliant and evil way that also involved a trip on I-5 and a violently carsick cat).

The other time I was greeted by cops on the morning shift was when it was time to leave Solano County Jail in 2004. I was older, but still stupid and much closer to actual addiction. I was driving home from a show I reviewed when I was a music writer. I drove up a steep hill on Interstate 80 that, typically, required my less-than-threatening Saturn to gain a certain amount of speed. The problem was there was a car doing 65 in the fast lane in front of me, and another doing 63 in the next lane. It was like they were holding hands trying to pull each other up the stupid hill.

So I impatiently cut across two lanes and passed them on the right in my car with the horsepower of a roller skate, stepping on it to get up the stupid hill separating Vallejo from Cordelia, where I lived. I'd been careful and didn't feel inebriated at all. I had a few drinks at the club in San Francisco (they gave me drink tickets and wouldn't I be insulting management, the owners, and all four bands on the bill if I didn't use them?). I'd been driving near the speed limit the whole trip home and was just about to wrap up another night at work. I'd also sat in my car before I left and ate two hot dogs from a street vendor, which everyone knows soaks up the booze (not really) and makes you sober (apparently not).

But when you impatiently cut across two lanes of traffic and speed up - even if you're barely going 70 but passing cars on the right - you get the attention of the California Highway Patrol. Which I did.

So we had the conversation: "Do you know why I pulled you over?" (Because you didn't play enough on your high school football team and became a cop?) "Do you know how fast you were going" (slightly faster than the 102-year-old person doing 65 in the fast lane?). "Have you been drinking tonight?" (define 'drinking?')

I didn't really say anything. I just blew in the breathalyzer -- a .10. Which was a couple molecules over the legal limit of .08. This was before my day drinking, when I was still productive at work, wasn't a slightly worse father than Jack Torrence in *The Shining*, and still had a first wife.

I was a homeowner. I owned a lawnmower. I went to Costco and bought potted trees for my yard. Yes, my job was spent going to concerts and clubs and bars. I still drank - but nothing compared to a decade later. Which is kind of like saying the massive earthquake that eventually led to the tsunami wasn't so bad in retrospect until tons of water started killing everyone.

I honestly didn't feel drunk - I couldn't have, because I remember every pleasant and exhilarating second of the experience, which mattered about as much as me saying so. I probably owed the state of California a couple thousand DUIs anyway, so I just shut up and got in the police car.

I did tell them, when offered the choice, I wanted to go to the hospital for a blood test instead of to the police station to get the official second breathalyzer reading that would be used in court. I figured it would take longer to get to the hospital, my blood alcohol level would drop, and perhaps I'd be lucky and a gang war would break out downtown and they'd be too busy to get to the quiet guy in the corner until he was legally sober. Then the policemen would admit the whole thing was just a big mistake, uncuff my hands to shake them in a friendly, apologetic fashion, and send me home to sleep. Maybe they'd escort me home, to make sure I arrived OK.

Like many ideas after I had a few, this one was bad. It took about 35 seconds to get to the hospital. They took me right into the lobby, where someone met us to take my blood. They're really good at this, I thought. Unfortunately, there was no serious crime in Solano County that night. Plus, the blood tests are deemed more accurate in court - I discovered later from some wiseass lawyer I got scared into hiring that it's much easier to fight the official breathalyzer at the police station than the blood test.

So I spent the night in the drunk tank, with five other guys - one of whom wouldn't shut up about how close he got to his driveway before the police got him and how unfair it was ... unfair that they just gave him his fourth DUI and he was probably going to San Quentin this time.

Dumbass. I may have been a drunk, but I usually knew whose fault it was.

No, none of it makes much sense. I just kept my mouth shut. I called my spouse collect and let her know I was in jail, in case she wondered. I think I made a file-in-a-cake joke I'm guessing she didn't find amusing. I spent the night in a room where going to the toilet meant going without a stall, about five feet away from your compatriots - which was a little disconcerting when some of the drunk stomachs got active.

The next morning, when they let us out, one of the cops recognized me as a guy from the newspaper, and announced it loudly (my press pass was in my wallet, so I'm guessing that's how he knew). By then I was totally and sadly sober and hadn't slept and couldn't even get angry and throw up on him. I just smiled and nodded and went out the door, waiting for my wife to pick me up for a really comfortable ride home. Then it just got better, when I walked into my house at 10 a.m. and my mother-in-law was standing there, looking at me, with Jesus probably standing right beside her (they went everywhere together), and my 2-year-old, asking where I'd been.

Daddy was in the big house, honey. The pokey. The slammer. Up the river, etc.

By Monday morning, I was getting unsolicited mail from every lawyer in the western United States, telling me I desperately needed them or my life was over. So I chose one, who charged me a couple thousand to do nothing he said he would and show up for court twice and say "thank you" to the judge. I got a fine, my license suspended for six months (which I ignored because I was invincible) and went to DUI school one night a week for six weeks (which I hated, but was nothing compared to the months of my life I'd spend in rehab later; I was just getting started). With my insurance adjusted, the whole thing cost me about ten grand the first year.

Those were some expensive free drink tickets.

As far as having cops over to my house without actually inviting them over, that was later in life, when I was drinking and driving from social events as a matter of course. I was still a couple years away from being able to say if I was conscious, I'd been drinking … but close enough. Definitely the "if the sun is down, the vodka's around" phase.

This time -- perhaps in 2010 -- I'd been over at a buddy's house, playing music with four friends. We were drinking, as usual. I apparently was drinking more. I don't remember if I got my drums in the car or left them there. I still have my drums, so they got home somehow. Maybe they took a cab.

But I do remember thinking I was going to sneak through town and take a back road home, instead of the freeway, where all those fellows from the California Highway Patrol were likely waiting to get me. I'd even drive right by the police station. No one expects an inebriated driver to try that, and I was very, very clever.

Except I was probably looking for cops looking for me (they did that) because I drove up the median RIGHT in front of the police station at a high rate of speed and just SLAMMED into it, hard enough to blow both front seat airbags. Which was, to say the least, a bit surprising. I have a feeling that woke me up - literally, since it was late, I'd played drums, and I was tired.

I mean, it probably wasn't the first time I woke up behind the wheel driving at a high rate of speed. But it was definitely the first time it involved exploding airbags.

So I woke up in the median and looked around. There were a couple cars here and there, but it was around midnight. No police cars.

I somehow gathered the parachute air-baggy things I didn't really understand at the moment, down from blocking my view through the windshield, and started rolling my crippled car up the road. The wheels were badly bent, my bumper was dragging, and I just wanted to get the last couple of miles home. That was the plan, anyway.

I made it. I parked my wounded Saturn in front of the house, decided I'd make up a story the next day, and went inside to go to bed. X2 was still awake. I went to bed and figured I was home and I was safe.

Wrong.

Someone saw me smash into the median and figured, accurately, that a guy who crashes his car in front of police headquarters and tries wobbling away with his airbags deployed, probably is having a stroke or has been drinking and is now driving, because the car – while listing like a torpedoed ship taking water on one side, was still moving. Or, at least attempting to move.

That person called 911 and, I assume, gave them my license plate number and said something to the effect of "Look for the slow-moving Saturn with two flats and a bent front end that looks like it was carjacked by a drunken crash test dummy."

Which, for the most part, I was. I'd crashed, I'd tested the police, and I was definitely a dummy.. Plus I probably didn't have a lot of life in my eyes. I just wanted to escape and get home.

A half hour to an hour later, there was a knock at our door. My wife answered and encountered two police officers inquiring as to the whereabouts of the driver of that giant crushed tin can out front.

Then she *let them come inside*. Which, eventually, infuriated me. Because the first rule of crashed car club is there is no inviting the police inside. That's like inviting the *Salem's Lot* vampire inside after you get a bloody nose.

I don't blame her. I imagine she was tired of dealing with my antics and decided if the police wanted a word with me, perhaps they should get it. So she escorted them to our bedroom, where they woke me up and asked what happened to my car.

I may have been lit (yes), and they may have gained entry into my home legally, but I was on the case. Before the days of breath-alyzers, I passed the field sobriety test six times; not once when I was actually sober. But I was great at the tests. Once a cop even pointed out it looked like something white was flaking from my nose. No sir, that's allergy medicine. Now, the last time I checked, you didn't sniff white powdered allergy medicine up your snout to make allergies go away, but some nights you just get on a roll.

I spent my share of quality time with police officers by 2009 or 2010 (whenever) when I sat up in bed, wondering why these barrel-chested people in black uniforms at the foot of my bed were looking at me.

I told them I hit a curb accidentally, but everything was fine and they should leave, because someone was probably robbing a bank or driving drunk downtown or something.

They said my car wasn't fit to be on a public road. I said I'd move it in the morning. They pointed out that wasn't exactly true unless I owned a tow truck. I didn't bother to point out how obvious it was that I was a masterful driver, considering I was in bed and there was half a bumper lying in the street in front of the police station three miles away.

They told me I should get up and at least show them my insurance information, which they said was likely in the car's glove compartment.

Nope ... too tired. Let's talk tomorrow. Come back - I'll make waffles.

They said I needed to come outside and show them my insurance and registration. They also said they got a call from a driver who witnessed my car hitting the median in front of the police station.

I said "Do you have a warrant to come inside my house?"

They said "That poor woman over there invited us in because she's sick of your stupid drunken antics. So we can legally be in your room and will probably pistol whip you if she asks nicely."

Well ... something like that.

I said "You won't arrest me If I go outside?"

They lied "No. What for?"

I laughed. I was wasted, but still wasn't stupid. Just stupid enough to drive drunk past the police station. I said something – or I meant to anyway -- that they couldn't prove that any alcohol I may have in my system was there when my car hit the curb in front of their stupid police station which, by the way, is ugly. I may have been sober all night and came home, drank a large barrel of vodka that's not here anymore, and went straight to bed.

"I'm not coming out unless you have a warrant," I said, thankful for TV police shows. I considered ending the sentence by calling them "coppers."

They said then they would have my car towed because it wasn't fit to be on a public street or something.

"Take it," I said, bravely (drunkenly) "I'm not coming out."

And I didn't … so they did. And that was the last time I ever drove that car.

I did get up to make sure they were gone. What was left of my car was definitely gone. I wasn't very pleasant to my then-wife, basically blaming her for setting me up … and probably a bunch of other things, including kidnapping the Lindbergh baby, Watergate, and the awful taste of gin.

She was upset, which made sense. I was an alcoholic dick. I just caused the police to come inside our home after midnight - I had no idea if any of our children saw - and now I was yelling about it in our front yard at 1 a.m.

It's shameful. Then it got worse the next day when I looked up how much replacing airbags would cost: More than what I could sell the entire car for.

I went back and forth with the crooked tow yard owner the following week. As the daily storage fees piled up, she always had an excuse as to why they couldn't release my car, even when I had money to get it. After four trips, the last to get my belongings, I told them to keep it. Which they did - then billed me for storing it for a month, a heavy chunk of money I had to pay off in installments. And I had to get a new car. Yes, after all that, I still didn't quit drinking. Quite the opposite.

I'm an idiot.

Chapter 5

You Have to Really Want It: Alcoholism is Hard Work

They call it being a functional alcoholic. Which is just a great way to say you may have a problem, but not in front of you and, besides, it's not really a problem since you totally got this non-problem under control, no problem.

My last couple of years with the second, and so far last, former Mrs.Hicks was a lot of work. Doubtless more for her than me, but she's not here sharing, so I can only speak for whoever lives inside my head at the moment. In fact, there's a tremendous amount of work involved in all aspects of being an alcoholic once you're years into it.

My work started first thing every morning when my eyes would open and I would, once confirming where I was physically, immediately target the location of my wife. If she was still asleep, I had options, depending on how much I drank the night before and how I felt.

If it was long enough before her typical waking up time - which meant the kids weren't awake - I had to decide whether I needed a trip to the liquor store, which opened at 6 a.m.. The early shift was manned by the store owner, who actually gave me credit from time to time when I had no cash. A merchant can do that when he's positive you're in his store at least once - frequently twice, sometimes thrice - per day.

Right - I bought in small quantities, as if it would be enough. I did this for years. I could probably buy a yacht with all the money I wasted.

If I judged it was going to be a bad morning physically, I could escape, come back with a caffeinated drink (and vodka, opened before I left the store parking lot and hidden in my car) and say something out loud to no one in particular, like "Boy, I knew I was going to need some caffeine today. Big, BIG day ahead!"

Of course, no one believed that shit. Most mornings my dog would roll his eyes at my 7-year-old, who would just shake her head back at the dog, who would look at the fish, who couldn't even look me in the eyes anymore.

Then I still had to ascertain whether I was in trouble or not (I was almost always in trouble, so this really came down to whether I was in *enough* trouble to hear about it that morning). Which I'll get back to momentarily.

The second option was that my then wife was waking up around the same time as me. In which case, I had choices, such as walking around, getting the kids up while trying not to throw up on them, starting the day, and ho-hum … just getting on with it.

Option three was to wait her out, ascertain the mood, and determine my response to her response to my actions of the previous night. Which, in most cases, I didn't remember - at least not the last hour or two of the evening.

Option four, and my least favorite, was when she was already up, or in the bathroom when I woke up. That was the most frightening. I'd usually lay paralyzed, fixated on the bathroom door. Because the second she walked out - and I saw her face - I could tell what happened the previous night, though usually not details, but at least the degree of bad.

Sometimes it was nothing. Sometimes her face was sad, or angry, or just disappointed or resigned, which was the worst.

Sometimes - very rarely - we'd talk about it. Almost always on those days, there was no "good morning" or any kind of greeting, which was pretty terrible (for me - I'm pretty sure it was even worse for her). However you slice it, it was always a bad way to start the day, selfishly trying to figure out how you hurt feelings or otherwise made your loved ones upset and/or angry the night before. And then concentrating on how to make everything seem like, if they're reacting to what I did, they're probably overreacting.

"Oh no, I was just tired, had a long day, had something on my mind, and had to go outside and into the garage 13 times last night while it was raining, because there's just a lot of stuff out there that needed organizing."

I did this six or seven mornings a week, 365 nights a year, for probably two or three years, at least. It was pretty exhausting for everyone.

As the child of a family whose father/grandfather drank and who spent their evenings habitually and recreationally arguing, I was no stranger to being on the other side of this ugliness. I frequently felt guilty because I knew how my kids felt. But not guilty enough to not let it happen again just hours later.

There was no real exit strategy that didn't involve professional help, and I really don't know what I was thinking, other than I felt like alcohol was oxygen and without it, I couldn't breathe. There was no planning and I felt bad for my family. But not enough to actually stop.

From what I could piece together, some nights I was angry. Some nights I wouldn't shut up. Some nights I overreacted and snapped at my kids for doing nothing more than being kids. Some nights I was giddy and would fixate on videos on YouTube or something equally stupid and meaningless, forcing them to watch videos or listen to music with me. Some nights I fell asleep in the family room at 9 p.m. mid-sentence. Some nights I disappeared early and crashed in bed, leaving the reading of books and basic getting kids ready for bed stuff to the other adult. And some nights I was perfectly normal, despite being legally inebriated.

Sometimes I couldn't get a handle on what happened the night before, or my wife's take on it. Which might leave me waiting for a phone call later in the day, when I could get a better read on her. Luckily, I usually started drinking again by then and could deal with the phone call much easier as Mr. Hyde, instead of rightfully-sensitive Dr. Jekyll.

Sometimes I wouldn't hear about it for days, or never. My ex-wife stuffed emotions more expertly, and often, than hotel maids stuffing pillows into new cases. Which is why when the emotions would appear, they'd accompany her smashing a bottle (no, not the VODKA!) or, in one case, a breathalyzer all over the parking lot in front of the neighbors during a fast-moving argument over whether I hid bottles in my luggage. It was a very inopportune time, as we were packing the car and preparing to spend six hours bunched together in said car on the way to Disneyland.

Yeah ... great trip, that one. Had I pulled over four hours in and started a conversation with a tumbleweed, I would've got more response. We split up more than eight years ago and we still haven't discussed, in person, getting divorced, so ...

Another issue for me was the vomiting. Which I realize sounds problematic.

It got that way later and, really, how do you throw up regularly without it eventually becoming somewhat problematic? During my marriage, it was mostly dry heaving. For a couple years, part of my morning routine was either throwing up or the aforementioned simulated throwing up.

As you can imagine, in a relatively small home with four other people inside, you can't just shut a bathroom door, groan and choke like you're being strangled by a gorilla, and maintain an air of routine. Bathroom doors aren't thick enough to keep in that kind of awfulness.

So I - under the pretense of getting the newspaper or scraping morning ice off a car, or whatever, - would excuse myself to the front yard, where I could snake over to the corner and briefly retch. If someone came outside - which rarely happened because who wants to watch someone retch? - I would just pretend that damned paper boy must've thrown our daily news in the bushes again. I would get no reaction, either way.

I never said I was fooling anyone. Which was, you know, embarrassing. Yet we kept repeating this ridiculous play acting for months at a time, if not years. I had this cute habit of deciding I needed an ice cream bar at 9 p.m. (I would rotate excuses, this one came up at least once a week). So I would need to get in my car and drive to the convenience (liquor) store, which luckily also sold ice cream bars. If only those things came in boxes and weren't illegal to be sold in anything but single servings.

Sometimes I just needed to take a walk - after 9 p.m., in winter, when it was raining.

One summer evening my family all went to the local ice cream place, which was literally two doors down from my regular liquor store. Some extended family was with us, and I was out of booze, so I figured there were enough people in the mix for me to get lost in the shuffle. Once everyone got inside Baskin Robbins, I literally sprinted into the liquor store, grabbed a pint, paid for it, inhaled it standing in the doorway of the store, threw it away, sprinted back to the ice cream place, and arrived just as it was my turn to order.

Seriously. Never heard a peep about that one.

Being that reckless demonstrated a few things. Yes, I was that desperate to drink. But at times it was a game and I was the odds-on favorite to win the imaginary trophy, at least in my mind. I was the alcoholic who always thought he was the smartest guy in the room, fooling everyone else when, in fact, some of "them" either stopped caring about my idiocy and refused to play the game, or just gave up on me entirely.

My biggest concern at the time seemed to be keeping both ends of the supply chain moving. Keep the full bottles coming in and the empty ones going out. Which was as problematic as throwing up while driving. Like the time my ex-wife and the kids tried to get a jump on holiday decorating by getting the old green and red bins out of the garage, only to open them and find empty vodka bottles. Which in some dysfunctional families, just comes with the holidays. But we were still pretending I didn't have a problem and this sort of thing was normal.

I wasn't there, so I don't remember how many there were. I only knew at some point the past ten-and-a-half months I'd cleverly hidden at least one, believing I had plenty of time to remove it when the coast was clear. Then, being an alcoholic, I forgot three minutes later. We do that. A lot.

Nevertheless, my plans for removing the day's evidence usually had to be as well-planned as getting it within drinking range to begin with. This was one way I wasn't going to be like the alcoholic with whom I grew up.

My grandpa used to drink in his truck, the garage, the job site, the bar, the backyard ... pretty much anywhere my grandmother wasn't. It was fairly routine to stumble onto his empties. He was also a very intelligent man who understood that he couldn't just throw his bottles in the garbage when the people from whom he was kidding himself into thinking he was hiding his drinking, could find them.

I loved my grandpa and, if not for the drinking, he was a wonderful guy. But drinking, by nature, just shoves people away from their families. Especially kids, who supposedly don't know better (but they do). So anytime I could get his attention was a big deal for me. This isn't the crybaby poor-me, I was made this way because of my family's part of the story. Let's be clear: I made myself into an alcoholic. It was a solo job. I certainly saw what it meant early in my life, but if anything, it should've warned me off. My biological father's invisible man performance while I grew up (there's your blame and still tender feelings, right there) made me promise myself to be present as a dad. Even if I wasn't because, you know, I'm a lying alcoholic untethered from reality. But at least that's what I thought. So why couldn't I avoid the same thing happening when I grew up?

The explanation is pretty simple: Because I loved drinking.

I loved drinking from the second I tried it as a kid. I loved how it made me feel, I loved how it made me brave. I loved the taste and how it made me forget everything I disliked about myself. I was healthy. I was brave, handsome, funny, intelligent … I loved everything about it. If anything, I always felt like I was born to drink. I still love it, I suppose. I mourn its absence like a dead loved one sometimes. I just can't do it anymore.

But, blithering aside, I loved the old guy and still wanted his attention.

Anytime I could get my grandfather to play catch, or take me somewhere, or come to my game or whatever, it was a big deal. In sixth grade, I remember my best friend was over, which was a big deal because my grandmother was never crazy about me having friends over. I think she was weary of the unpredictability of having an alcoholic in the house and generally embarrassed. Anyway, my grandpa asked my friend Bob - who is still a friend 46 years later - if he wanted a ride home.

Heck yeah, I said, hopping in the truck. We were taking Bob home, like regular people when a kid comes over to their house.

We pulled up in front of Bob's very nice house (first hot tub I was ever in) and - swear to God - his parents were standing on the driveway, arms around each other, pretty much waving as we drove up to his beautiful home at the end of a court. At least that's what I remember. The scene was so functional as to be terrifying to me. When I was little and I'd go to other kids' homes, and everyone was getting along, I thought there was something seriously wrong with that family. No joke.

Anyway, so Bob said goodbye, thanked my grandpa, opened the door ... and one empty bottle (Miller Highlight, I'm pretty sure), rolled out and exploded on the end of the driveway. Which started a chain reaction: another rolled out and exploded on the ground, then another.

Everyone stopped. I was ready to run into the nearby creek and drown myself.. My grandpa sort of looked over at what happened, and didn't look too concerned (think Randy Quaid breaking the toy windmill in *Christmas Vacation*). Bob looked at me, then we both looked at his parents, who'd frozen, mid-wave (I'm probably making that up, but it sure felt that way). An hour (two seconds) passed.

"Oh ... we'll get that, no problem. Thanks for bringing Bob home."

They *said* that. Or something like that. My grandpa shrugged, Bob got out of the truck, everyone waved and we pulled away. And I wished I was dead.

By the way, after I wrote that, I reminded Bob of the story, which he didn't remember. Though he admitted it's possible. So I don't know … I wasn't drinking yet in sixth grade, and my long-term memory functions much better than my short-term brain. I'm positive it happened.

Despite my upbringing - during which there was lots of great stuff, too - I had so many hiding places in my car for empties, it's literally a miracle history never repeated itself. My kids found bottles periodically and I'd blame it on the neighbors, or that drunk Santa Claus, or a family member, or the neighbors' cat … whatever. They weren't stupid, yet alcoholics still treat kids that way. But I was still very aware of my empties because of that scene in front of my sixth grade BFF's house in 1979.

Plus I have an issue no one had in 1979. I might be an alcoholic. But I'm an anal-retentive recycling super*freak* of an alcoholic. Even sober, I'm completely disorganized, have no idea if I've paid my taxes, don't remember when my bills are due, and think I now owe more than three times what I actually received in student loans … I haven't checked in a while. I don't remember my address most days and haven't looked at my day calendar in months.

But I *do not* mess around when it comes to recycling. I mean, if a micron of plastic falls off something, I do everything but pull a magnifying glass from my pocket to find it and make sure it's secured in the recycling bag.

I could live with being a shitty husband and father and a less-than-stellar employee, and a drunk driver and liar. But I was just racked with guilt over humankind's treatment of the Earth unless I think I'm somehow saving it by recycling. It's another way I'm just another ridiculous suburban white man. I couldn't just toss empties in bushes, or in a public garbage can, or down a sewer or something. I would have *nightmares*.

Well … OK. That's not true. I did all those things, because sometimes getting rid of the evidence trumps anal-retentive tree-hugging. But I felt really bad about it.

I even had a favorite can: the one in the parking lot of the YMCA, which had one of those long extensions, so you didn't even have to exit your car when tossing empties. It was like a reverse drive thru. On weekends I'd wake up, have a drink to make myself feel normal, go to the gym, lay on the men's room floor dry-heaving quietly so I didn't disturb my fellow club members (sometimes I'd park in the corner of the lot farthest from the door so I could just throw up in peace), work out, possibly throw up in the parking lot again afterwards (it somehow made sense), then scrounge up the bottles I'd hidden in my car the previous week and dispose of them through the drive-thru garbage can.

But I was still an alcoholic who loved Mother Earth and there-fore loved recycling. I pull labels off bottles of juice when my kids are done with them because I suspect the recycling police won't process the bottle if there's still paper on it. I'm rarely anal retentive about anything because being anal retentive doesn't really go with being a successful, functional alcoholic (success being objective in this scenario, of course). But I've been known to get mad at seeing someone put a plastic water bottle into the gym garbage can and actually march over and pull it out of the trash.

Speaking of plastic water bottles, those are some of the most useful, best friends a successful functional alcoholic has. Because obviously you can't drag a big bottle of vodka around with you everywhere you go. I mean, you could, but then people stop inviting you to their kids' birthday parties.

I, like so many alcoholics, believed at some point I was the first genius to start putting my vodka in an empty water bottle. Then you go to rehab or AA and get mad because you discover all these stupid alcoholics stole your idea. But water was my second favorite drink, and it was the same color as my first favorite. So that's where I kept my vodka. Of course, I'd frequently have a mothership bottle hidden somewhere, because buying in large quantities is just smart alcoholic shopping. Being an alcoholic gets expensive. I probably averaged $20 a day in vodka, which wasn't easy making journalist money. Yeah … probably $600 a month. And that doesn't count buying drinks when you go out. I mean, I wasn't thinking about that when I married my second ex-wife, but it didn't hurt that she made more money than me. I probably spent more than 10 percent of my salary on alcohol those years. Not to mention the emotional cost, which was far too great for a price tag.

Right. Alcoholism is really, totally awful. But I believe there's almost always a way out of it, as long as you aren't dead yet. Unfortunately - or fortunately - people can lower you as many ladders as will fit into the hole you dug yourself. You just usually won't come out until you find your own way. And, for some of us, that means getting really dirty and frequently sliding back through all that heavy mud and gravity until the hole is about to collapse on us. Then we realize we really have to get to work or get buried alive.

Chapter 6

Tony, You Can Drive My Car

At some point in 2018 (or 2019 - whatever, same decade), someone took a giant cheese grater to the right side of my dark blue 2013 Nissan Rogue when I was probably off feeding hungry children or building homes for disadvantaged hurriquake victims in a far away land.

Either that or I crashed my car.

It wasn't actually much of a crash. I'd done more damage to cars on purpose. It was still drivable and nothing was dragging or scraping or half-functional (I, however, was a different story). There was a dent and some missing paint, suspiciously all the shape of one of those underground concrete pillars in the Target parking lot.

I just went with it because, obviously, how your car looks is pretty far down the list of priorities when you're 51, living with your parents, unemployed, drinking all three meals every day, and your children are terrified of you.

I had a varied history with cars. I'd technically totaled one, the night the police tried to get me out of bed. Years earlier, I smashed another one into a rockslide going up the Grapevine in a storm. I drove Chevy Novas (two) through guardrails, gates, park benches, front yards, mailboxes, fences … and hundreds (seriously) of garbage cans. I was in the front seat of a Trans Am that crashed into the front of a house while in high school.

We weren't drinking, I wasn't driving and it wasn't my fault - I didn't even have my license yet. But a guy who grew up in the 70s doesn't crash into a house in a Trans Am, write a book, and not say something when talking about car crashes.

Of course, all these incidents took years of careful planning. Crashes frequently happened on purpose because I liked attention. I liked being *that* guy, the one winning $20 bets with people over whether I could drink a bottle of Jack Daniels in one gulp.

Therefore, I was very familiar with the damage on my right front quarter panel and door. I wasn't familiar with the memory of doing it. But I knew I did something. The car still moved and, if anyone asked, I said a pack of animals attacked me on a dark road or something. Big deal.

Except my ex-wife finally noticed the damage when we were doing a hostage (my daughter) exchange one day. And she remembered that, while I made the car payments and drove the thing for five years, it was technically in her name, because her credit was better than mine in 2014 (I'm guessing it still is).

Soon afterward, I'd had a bad week at my mom's house and decided to spend a few days in a cheap hotel, living the good (bad) life in a shaky part of Concord, California. Because day drinking like Charles Bukowski in a really really bad mood, in front of my 70-something parents, was kind of a non-starter. I don't think they actually called the police on me yet, but there'd been threats.

I certainly wasn't in the mood to stop drinking, or look for a job, or make myself useful, so I spent four or five days at a motel watching TV and seeing if I could get my liver to float.

Right. I was being very constructive and unshakably logical.

I only left to refill at a nearby liquor store with a catchy name like "Liquors R Us!" or "Cheap and Easy" or something. A more accurate name would've been "Spend $25 Here and Instantly Make Cheap Motels Look Way Better."

Inevitably, I finally fell apart and called my mom, who sent my aunt to come get me. I cried on the drive home and the Nissan Rogue stayed behind. And, perhaps not coincidentally, there was a conversation around that time between my mom and her ex-daughter-in-law about my driving skills and her liability.

So she repo'd my car, I believe from the motel, though I wasn't entirely sure. I do know there was a previous attempt at repo involving her and a friend of ours who was going to drive it back to my former residence. Which upset my mom, because she wasn't already upset enough with me.

In my family, we can drink ourselves to near death, scream, hit each other with wooden door stoppers shaped like cats (true story) or light each other's reading material on fire when that person is still reading it (also true). But outsiders are verboten to even blink with anything but the most honorable intent in our general direction, at least according to my mom.

I love my mom very much, by the way. Throughout my years of irresponsibly and prematurely aging her, she was the only person who didn't give up on me, when basically everyone else did. My kids don't count, because they're really good people who were too young to understand the damage I caused. I had a few friends who were usually there for me, but they didn't have to live with me acting worse in my 40s and 50s than we did in our 20s. Otherwise, most of my friends escaped my burning house of a personal life; usually for good reasons. My mom may have called the police, threatened me, had me committed (briefly), and screamed at me … but she never gave up on me. She probably should've and she likely enabled me at times. But she didn't give up. Ever.

I didn't just burn bridges over those years. I poured gasoline over gunpowder on them, then hit them with a flamethrower coming from a Sherman tank.

I was car-less and careless. And my mom loved me, so against all common sense, she let me drive her car.

Of course it was a mistake. Things started breaking almost immediately. The car was 20 years old - a convertible red Mustang. The roof started malfunctioning immediately and I accidentally scraped a neighbor's car, shearing the right side mirror right off (maybe not technically, as I glued and duct taped it back on). I was actually sober when I did it, which was weird.

In fact, I was so sober, I was going through a startlingly strange phase of honesty, thanks to all those AA meetings/indoctrinations, and actually told the neighbors what I did to their Mercedes (of course it was a Mercedes).

As far as my mom's car, at various times I broke a key off in the trunk and broke another off in the ignition, requiring a locksmith to somehow rig the steering column at my kid's softball game so I could still start it with a half-key. I also slammed the rear end into a concrete pillar that wasn't at Target, also when sober (right, I seem to be building a case I drive better drunk). Basically, either

I was destroying the car or it was falling apart on its own as soon as someone started driving it regularly. Mom is half-blind, hasn't been on a freeway in decades, and only put about 40,000 miles on it. Which is what I racked up the next three years.

But transportation wasn't the real value of that car. That came into play when the car became my shelter.

Having no place to live is much like getting arrested: it feels terrible and helpless and is probably something everyone should encounter, even briefly. I'm not actually recommending either. Especially when one is sobering up. Cops, in my experience, treat humans in their "care" worse than farmers treat livestock. And I'm a safe (relatively) suburban white male they're not institutionally (and frequently wrongly) classifying a criminal as soon as they see me.

I've been arrested four times and incarcerated three times. And twice I've been physically accosted by police. I'm a wiseass, to be sure, but I know there's no percentage in popping off around cops. Which is why I've escaped so many DUIs. That and the fact that I used to be very skilled while keeping my balance and counting backwards.

One time I was pushed against a wall while wearing handcuffs. But that was in L.A. right after the Rodney King verdict, and I figured the cops were just trying to prove they were assholes to people of all colors (I went to jail for peacefully protesting, not looting). The other time was a couple years ago, when I left a holding cell in a certain Contra Costa County city a bit battered and definitely bruised. I was a 50-something confused suburban white man they felt the need to strike with the end of a nightstick a couple times. I was detoxing, confused and about as threatening as a cocker spaniel on nitrous oxide. I have my theories as to why - I believe one of the nice officers knew who I was, because he was close friends with a man who didn't like me dating his ex-wife (which I get, but still). Whether that had anything to do with me getting slammed against a wall more than once and struck in the chest hard enough to bruise is just speculation. Big deal. But everytime I see police departments posting photos on their official Facebook pages of girl scouts baking them cookies or people otherwise bestowing sainthood on them, I usually think "Now there's a person who's never been to jail." Because it's a learning experience.

No. I don't want girl scouts to go to jail. And I have to look at cops' social media because it's part of my job. The point is experience, even bad experience, matters. If you really want to learn about someone, see how they behave when they have you at their mercy.

Same for homelessness. This was one of my biggest fears, going back to hearing about homelessness as a kid and not believing we let people not have homes. Not in the United States. It was scary to me.

Even as a 50-year-old, the first time it was suggested to me my behavior might lead to stepdad Bob kicking me out of his home was just unimaginable. People don't do that to each other. Not around here and not to me. I was someone. People recognized me in public.

I sat in the good seats at concerts. I had rock stars' numbers in my phone. I was pretty sure I was kind of a big deal.

I was homeless probably for 10 or 12 nights, over a year, maybe more; I wasn't counting. And here are the biggest lessons I learned from my brief bout of housing insecurity: If you were sane when you became homeless, you won't remain that way for long. Not having the security of a place to call home rips away part of your emotional foundation and the longer you stay that way, the less likely it is to recover that emotional security.

The other lesson is: Homelessness is a LOT of work.

I thought being an alcoholic was a lot of work - and it was. And I was totally good at it for a long time. But even being homeless in the relatively safe suburbs means your head is on a swivel. The police are not typically your friends, so you're on constant alert. You don't want to stay in one place too long so someone doesn't start questioning what the hell you're doing and calls the police. You become neurotic and nothing about it is pleasant, smell included.

So you're always moving around, and always looking for a safe space where you can let your guard down. When you run out of money, you steal food. In my case, I stole food and booze, which is convenient when you wake up behind 7-Eleven. You can't leave your belongings because you're afraid someone will steal them. And there's no Netflix when you're homeless (unless you're much better at homelessness than I was).

When you don't have a lot of money, but need money to drink, and need to drink to live, strange things happen that strangely don't seem strange at all because you live in a twilight zone where colors aren't as colorful and everything feels strangled and frantic. I once threw up in my mom's car right in the liquor store parking lot after I had my first drink of the day. Which felt like such a waste because it was the first quarter of the bottle and, in my dehydrated, inside out brain, felt like pouring out the first quarter of the bottle and wasting it. It was like burning money. Years before, liquor became currency. Finding a half-full bottle you forgot was like finding a wad of cash on the sidewalk.

So I wiped my mouth, took a second to reset, then drank again. It wasn't the first, or last, time that happened. That car took such a beating.

The first time I was thrown out with nowhere to go, my aunt - and I have no idea how she got involved - dropped me off at a homeless shelter in Concord. Which I thought was better than sleeping outside.

I thought wrong. Now I know why homeless people stay away from shelters.

This shelter was a room in an office park. There was some old furniture set around a TV. You were not allowed to lay down (not kidding). There were signs everywhere warning you not to leave your things unattended. I don't think people were allowed to have more than a backpack.

I don't remember what was on TV, but it wasn't Netflix. You were allowed to sit up, squeezed next to other people, in front of the

TV. We all smelled amazing. I don't remember any cots or designated sleeping areas, but there's a real possibility I was hallucinating. People slept sitting up, wedged between other people. I didn't sleep at all, because I was obviously having too much fun. And once the sun was up the party was over; you were out. Period. You didn't even get coffee and doughnuts.

That was my last night in a shelter. I'd rather be jammed into a car, alone and under my own incredibly responsible supervision. It's not even close.

I spent nights behind a 7-Eleven that was kind of tucked away. I spent a few nights in the car in a corner of the Safeway parking lot in which I grew up riding my bike with my friends, right outside Rossmoor in Walnut Creek, CA. It wasn't far from my mom's and about a mile from where I grew up.

Strangely, I somehow felt attached to that spot. I don't know, maybe it felt a bit comfortable during a situation when nothing else was. I spent a lot of time in that parking lot - when we were 10 or 11 years old we discovered there was an elevator in the old-fashioned strip mall and, for some reason, that became very exotic to us. We felt like roughnecks breaking the law when we would take our bikes inside the elevator and go up and down (to *both* floors) nine or 10 times. Right - no cell phones or computers in the 1970s. There was also a bank there that gave out free summertime ice cream a couple times, which was even bigger news than the elevator. I was parking my (mom's) car for the night about 40 yards from where an old buffet restaurant named Piper's used to be, where my family occasionally went on very special occasions. The idea of a kid taking a tray and getting to choose what hot food to eat, from a family in which it was law to eat well-done meat and baked potatoes every night, was like a digestive amusement park.

I sort of felt safe there … for as much as one can feel safe while having nowhere to sleep but a 20-year-old car. I kind of felt my grandparents - with whom I lived until I was 12 - and my small gang of white boy wanna-be tough guys on dirt bikes - were still somewhere around there. I know I smiled a bit more those nights. I snuck into Starbucks every morning and pretended to drink coffee while charging my phone.

I know what you're thinking, but living in an old car isn't as glamorous as it's cracked up to be.

Typically, whatever you own that isn't in storage is stuffed in there with you. Changing clothes in that much space can cause screaming cramps (yay - claustrophobia!). Finally, you risk being seen and jump out of the car to change your clothes standing up in a parking lot, hoping to God no one sees you and calls the (not) very sympathetic police. The garbage produced by any food you eat may stay in the car for a while, because you're keeping a low profile - so trips outside, like to a garbage can, are minimized. And, of course, it's cold. If you're in a convertible that's nearly old enough to drink, the roof is bound to leak somewhere. For once, I was thankful for a drought. But it was fall and winter, so I did get rained on a bit. I had some towels to set under the leaks.

Bathrooms? Yeah, great question. Part of that is usually no problem, as California has trees, The other part … I honestly don't remember. I think I held it a lot. Which didn't really solve the problem. Luckily I wasn't eating much. My drinking had evolved to the point where when I did so, that's all I did. I didn't eat. I went from 220-230 pounds, typically, to the 170s by 2019. Throwing up was such a regular thing by then, it no longer fazed me at all - though it was a little awkward when still driving. When I was sober and skinny, people told me I looked great. Which usually made me smile, not necessarily at the nice compliment, but at the raw ignorance of people automatically believing less weight was worth compliments when my liver was screaming at them and their compliments to fuck off. Though I only knew better the hard way - which was, and is, pretty much the main way I learn things. I'm the guy who never learns until he teeters on disaster.

I'll tell you one thing I learned: Being homeless numbed by alcohol and/or drugs sure beats the hell out of dealing with homelessness sober, though. I will never give a homeless person a couple dollars on the idiotic condition they stay sober. I don't know how homeless people don't drink, even if I finally stopped long enough to get back into my mom's house or, in a couple cases, a sober living house. I did five months in two of those and discovered I'm too old for sharing bedrooms, mandatory AA meetings, and people younger than me ordering me to do chores. It's great for some people; it didn't really work for me. But I'm a stuck-up jerk.

Some nights my mom would meet me a few houses down from

her place to give me food and whatever else she thought I needed. I wasn't allowed anywhere near the house. A good friend and former coworker - who previously tried to be my sponsor - took me to AA meetings and fed me. He also let me sleep on his covered patio room for a few months. He was great to me, but I finally drank my way out of his house just as I sobered up some and he was offering me a real room to rent. I think what did him in was the Saturday afternoon I drank and spent the afternoon moaning until the neighbors called the police. Twice.

I was just moaning. I guess I was in pain. I certainly wasn't happy, and moaning felt like exercising the pain from my system. I don't remember much about that day, though I do remember thinking about a couple people in my life that pained me enough to make me sit there and moan (yeah - daddy stuff, which my sisters weren't happy about when I started firing them texts). It was weird. I lacked all emotional control. Even after the cops came and told my friend to shut me up, I did it again. And they had to come back. I don't know how he kept them from hauling me to the psych ward, but I am forever grateful to him for his kindness.

It was at his house I first decided to give up. I was detoxing and trying to straighten up when, about two days in, my legs just stopped working. I previously had this problem before Christmas 2017 when I spent six days in the hospital and there was a suggestion from a doctor that maybe I had a stroke (of course, after they could accurately test me for it, they said, but I heard that second hand).

I walked across his house to use the bathroom and my legs just gave out, forcing me to crawl back to the couch on which I was living. I'd try again and get a few feet and collapse again. I finally stopped being able to get up.

I was really scared. I had a headache and my limbs weren't working. Then I strangely calmed down. I figured I was having a stroke and that was probably it for me. I decided against calling for help - I'd been in ambulances at least four times between 2017 and 2019, which didn't count the times someone drove me to the hospital, and I was tired of them. I was tired of the looks from the doctors who didn't want to treat me. I was tired of being a pain in the ass. I was tired of disappointing and angering people. I figured if I was having a stroke, I could just do so here and die.

I didn't. Which was, you know, good.

I gradually got better as I had somewhat of a (brief) revelation that maybe I needed a higher power after all. I didn't really find one, but just being open to the possibility helped. For a while I tried talking to whatever higher power might be in the neighborhood and interested, which may have helped me process what the hell I was doing. It took me a couple days until I could walk right again. I asked my doctor about it and he looked at me like I just pulled a Big Mac out of my rear end.

Actually, that's not true. Other people looked at me like that, but my doctor - whom I consider a friend - has been with me for 27 years and he's heard it all, but he didn't have any concrete answers. Falling down when you're drunk is one thing, but when you stop drinking for a few days … I guess I was right and I really am special.

When I left my friend's patio, it was holiday time again and, without a walker this time, managed to talk my way back into my parents' house. I went to a lot of AA meetings, did some freelance writing, and tried staying sober. I got to the point where I was ready to move into a new place after nine months.

My daughter, who was back from Florida, 18 years old, and living with her dying grandmother about 40 miles away, came to live with me. My former mother-in-law - a wonderful lady with whom I kept in contact the previous 15 years I wasn't married to her daughter (she always prayed for me because she knew I needed it) - finally succumbed to cancer after suffering through it for years.. It was about the same time I moved into my first real home, one that was mine all mine, in more than three years. My newfound ability to stand up without falling over - at least enough to work and get my own place again - was very timely. Just when my daughter needed me, which really helped keep me sober for the next year.

That was also five months into the COVID-19 lockdowns. It was funny how the pandemic freaked everyone out to the point where the day drinking numbers soared. I actually (mostly) got sober during the pandemic, which was weird but certainly par for the course for me, since I can't seem to do anything how I'm supposed to. I couldn't even day drink when the rest of the country decided it was acceptable.

So after one last brief three-day binge that got me kicked out again (HA! Joke's on you; I'm leaving anyway) my daughter and I moved to a very small apartment in a very nice neighborhood. I got a fulltime job and stayed sober for a year. Then, as I mentioned earlier, I discovered the girl I loved - who I hadn't seen in a year - was done waiting for me and was dating someone else. Which somehow surprised me, even though I frequently wasn't very nice to her over the course of our strange three-year ... whatever it was. I had this idea that, since she didn't trust me, I'd stay sober for a year, then see about reconciling. Of course, I didn't tell her that was the plan and, apparently, she had her own. As I should've expected, but everything was still all about me.

So I don't really remember the next five days. I was still driving my mom's car, so this time it was my daughter confiscating the keys instead of my mom. By then I'd developed a funny little habit whenever I drank: I disappeared from social media and work and drank for five to seven days, until I realized I was going to die if I continued.

Only this time, I do remember consciously deciding I was going to drink myself to death. It seemed the easiest thing to do. I was tired, heartbroken, and more than OK with that. This is where the insanity of alcoholism comes in.

I'd been sober for a year. I finally had a job in my field I could keep and make enough on which to live. My daughter was back from her awful misadventures in Florida and back in California, initially struggling to find a place to live and being taken in by her grandmother while her stupid father flailed in alcoholism, only to watch her grandma get sicker and finally die. She'd been through a lot. But, in theory, we were back on track … and I was seemingly pissing it away.

Not only that, but I was such a selfish bastard, I was doing it all in front of my then 19-year-old. My then 13-year-old also witnessed the beginning of my binge, so her sister took her home in an Uber because Dad was no longer able to drive the other grandma's car.

Why? What the hell could possibly tear me down that fast when I was so close?

It wasn't about lost love. It was because I decided to drink, and nothing was going to stop me. Explosives couldn't have stopped me. Because, though I had a year of sobriety behind me, I hadn't prepared. I hadn't dealt with the underlying issues that kept me in a state of "dry" drunkenness. My process, when things didn't go well, was to immediately drink without even trying anything else.

And once I had one drink, I was gone for days. Every time. It was the bottom of the bottom, which I'll never forget, even if I don't really remember. When I drink, my accomplishments, my job, my relationships, pretty much everything, just vanishes.

My daughter finally had enough on or around day five when, since she took my keys, I tried to walk to the store. As I stepped outside, she grabbed me and guided me back in the house. I hadn't eaten in days and she offered to make me some food. Which sounded really nice. Of course, I wasn't wearing pants, so she correctly figured she should intervene. Strolling around upscale downtown Lafayette in my drawers probably would've earned me another trip to jail.

The food tasted so good. I think it was a kindness as small as my kid offering to make me some silly frozen pizza that just did me in. I cried that night. I'd become a serious, doctoral-level expert on isolation and loneliness, which was partly because drinking is much easier alone by then and partly because no one really wanted to be around me anymore, because I was either embarrassing or miserable or embarrassingly miserable.

Put those parts together and it adds up to one guy's fault. Which I'm OK with ... or at least getting better with.

I still drove that car for another year until it finally, kind of like the Bluesmobile in *The Blues Brothers*, just laid down and died. But it was a beautiful car despite how badly it was beaten up. It was literally a lifesaver, and I thanked it profusely before the tow truck hauled it away.

Chapter 7

Stories I Never Wrote

I was out on a story last year for my latest employer when the subject of my old newspaper came up.

Hiking on the north flank of Mt. Diablo in a group including a local state assemblywoman there for the photo opp, one of the people I interviewed actually asked whatever happened to that guy who used to write columns about his kids and music and movies and other distracting mush.

Yeah, that was me, I said, apparently modestly but secretly excited because a stranger still remembered. Then I mumbled some slippery jargon about "the business" and "the modern media landscape," or whatever, when he asked why I'm not writing witty little things about my darling children anymore.

Then I changed the subject and wished my water bottle was full of vodka, just like the bad old days.

I, of course, never tell the truth, which isn't true. Which I guess I'm doing now, hoping someone remembers - maybe me - I was the guy who not-very-magically made himself disappear.

It was no surprise when my life melted down in 2017. I knew the marriage was over. I knew my friends didn't invite me to gatherings anymore because what used to be funny in our 20s terrified everyone's wives in our 40s. It was still weird. Being the guy who drinks too much for my friend group was like being the guy shunned at the NRA convention for being the crazy gun nut.

And I knew my career, as I'd known it, was over. Well … sort of. I knew the career I knew was over, though that acceptance was a mighty giant wall for a weighty ego to scale. That may have been the hardest part. Because, while I didn't make a lot of money (they paid us in used vegetables) my job made me feel like a big deal for a bit.

No, they didn't *always* pay us with vegetables. I told you - alcoholics lie. Though they did give us $10 Safeway gift cards one year for holiday bonuses, about which the underpaid people just smart enough to go into journalism openly laughed in front of management. Or maybe that was just me.

But I knew what I was getting into. I did something I loved that got me a measure of respect and free drinks. Even the people who constantly wrote to the paper to say I sucked were at least paying attention. Which I liked.

But my last couple years at the newspaper weren't great. I was unhappy. About five years before I left, our big brother newspaper to the south, owned by the same company, moved in like the star destroyer sucking up Princess Leia's ship in the beginning of *Star Wars*.

Almost immediately I knew my career as a section front columnist was over. A honcho editor from the mothership, who took himself way too seriously and laughed too loudly at his own jokes, decided I wasn't going to be a columnist anymore. Which was upsetting, because - as flawed as some of the work was - much of my identity was tied up in that work. And some of it was pretty good, according to my pets and young children.

I can admit now I was terrified. My whole identity, for a while anyway, was that smirking guy atop the left hand column of the newspaper twice a week. It was the job for which I believed I gave up being a music writer and I thought if I lost that, I'd lose everything (which actually happened, but not for the reasons I thought).

Of course, as I wasn't reacting well, my drinking - which was already heavy for humans - got even heavier. And I'd been drinking almost nightly for more than a decade.

It wasn't the newspaper's fault I was careening my career Big Wheel downhill toward the busy alcoholic highway. It was just an excuse to rely on the alcohol even more. I mean, I went on to become a movie critic and pop culture writer. I got paid to make fun of the Kardashians. It wasn't like I was cleaning toilets at an elementary school anymore (I was 22 and needed the money).

I still felt lost. And my heart was no longer in the job - a failure on my part, because it was up to me to find the meaning in what I did. There was more than enough opportunity. I was just too caught up in what I was losing - which really wasn't much. But it was the excuse I took to drink more.

It progressed. While my marriage spiraled, the last two years at the paper, I missed assignments. I got sick more and more. I missed deadlines. In the biggest professional embarrassment of my life - which is really saying something, since I once gave a glowing review to Metallica's *St.Anger* - I was the movie writer who disappeared the night of the Oscars' biggest controversy in modern history, at least until Will Smith started slapping people. They announced the wrong movie winning the best picture Oscar, and I was probably dozing or microwaving a bagel dog because I forget to eat that day.

I just assumed I was fired after missing the academy putting the wrong movie in the best picture envelope. I woke up and still - lamely - wrote a story at 4 a.m. that was perfunctory and unnecessary at best. I should've packed my things and moved to a different state. But no one really said anything, which was really weird.

I think my supervisors were like others who knew me and hoped the better version would reappear, only to be repeatedly disappointed. Big indicators of my work problems showed on two occasions I dedicated time and travel to interview two important people on my beat for stories that should've been good, that would've excited me a few years earlier. I showed up for both interviews, asked questions, took notes ... and never wrote the stories.

Nope, no real idea why. It certainly wasn't a conscious decision. I just may have been too busy trying to slowly kill myself.

The first big swing and miss was on a Disneyland trip. I'm an embarrassing Disneyland freak. The Magic Kingdom and Santa Cruz were the vacations my family took when I was a kid. So I love both and go as often as possible. My family wasn't super happy when I was a kid, but things were different there. At least for me. At the top of my family food chain was a talented, alcoholic grandfather probably suffering from undiagnosed PTSD from World War II - back when they didn't allow ideas like PTSD, so suffering veterans just drank themselves to death. Next to him was my unhappy grandmother, who loved me like crazy but was severely disappointed with how life turned out. But Disneyland was always a parade of great memories. So when I got old enough to have a career and write occasionally for the travel section, I was usually first in line for the Disneyland stories. Because it was a great excuse to brainwash my kids into loving Disneyland for free. Taking a family of five to Disneyland wasn't cheap. So Disney's PR people would pitch something and I'd gobble those free tickets - and sometimes free hotel rooms - right up.

From what I remember - and that usually isn't much - I did at least four and maybe five Disneyland travel stories in my years at the newspaper. I miss those times; it was nice to take my kids somewhere like that and get treated well.

For the last one in 2015 or 2016 - right before the career and marriage ended, the Disney media relations guy asked me if I wanted to have a face-to-face with the Disneyland boss. It wasn't the CEO, whose name everyone usually knows. But there was a C in his title, and he was supposed to be a big deal.

To this day, I don't remember his name. I swear to God. I'm pretty sure I knew it then, or at least wrote it on my hand or something, in case I needed it.

But I got my sit-down with him. It was in the middle of a day in May or June and I wasn't drinking yet. I got to sit on the patio of Walt Disney's old apartment, above the Main Street fire station. Which is like sacred ground to Disney nuts. I was very excited - Walt Disney's patio!

I tried being very professional. I asked him about the future of the park. They'd bought the *Star Wars* franchise from George

Lucas, so I immediately asked if that meant a *Star Wars* land in the park (which eventually happened, called Galaxy's Edge, which is pretty awesome). He wouldn't comment so, bingo! - I had something to work with. A smiling no comment on building a *Star Wars* land which, of course, meant they were totally planning one (This was still before they released Disney's first *Star Wars* film - *The Force Awakens*, which came soon after. I didn't bother asking much about the film - because as a *Star Wars* freak and pop culture and film writer, I'd been on high alert all year, and no one at Disney was talking).

It was a good, professional interview. I worked a few angles, including one about ticket prices recently going up. I asked him point blank how regular American families could afford going to Disneyland with these astronomical prices. I expected him to feed me some swill about programs to get low-income families into the park, or scholarships, or raffles … or California property values, or having to pay for the next 300 generations of George Lucas' descendants to go to college. Something …

Instead, he looked over the railing at the tons of people entering the park below at the entrance onto Main Street, and said something to the effect of "Apparently people can afford it, because the park is full. Every day. So they are finding ways."

It was kind of a gross answer, but honest. Which I sort of respected. The capitalist swine had a point.

Still, the statement stood on its own for the obvious arrogance, which would be good for my story. I wasn't necessarily pursuing that angle until he handed me something really good to work with. I asked a few more questions, wrapped up my 20 minutes or whatever, finished my tea, and was escorted back down to mix with the sweaty masses. I was excited ... I had a great story to work with.

Some editor somewhere may still be waiting for it.

I wrote my main story about what Disneyland was doing that summer - I couldn't get away with not doing that one, or I'd never get to go back without paying (and certainly won't now). I may have been a psychotic drunk, but I wasn't about to kill the golden mouse. But the good story for which I actually practiced some real journalism for about 20 minutes? Never did it. I honestly don't know why. I wasn't drinking that day; I still sometimes waited for the sun to go down back then. I just didn't do it. I don't think I cared enough anymore ... about anything.

The other insane example of a story I didn't write, but spent a half work day traveling to San Francisco and back was in 2016, when Michael Moore released "Where to Invade Next," which I know I reviewed, because I just looked it up on the Internet.

Moore did a press junket to promote the movie - which Rotten Tomatoes says I liked - and I had the usual interview in a nice San Francisco hotel (no idea where this one was - though quite a few were at the Fairmont).

Because I'm a recycling, small mammal-loving, climate change worrying, tree-fondling, free-the-orcas, fruitbag socialist, I'm a fan of Moore's movies ... within reason. He has an agenda, he sometimes drags people through the mud and ... well, that's about it. He's smug but very smart, and I was looking forward to our conversation.

And it was a great conversation, from what I recall. I also remember he had more junk food on the coffee table than I'd seen in an entire grocery store. It was like he attacked three really large vending machines and scattered the wrappers around the room to warn any meandering fruits and vegetables they weren't welcome. Maybe it was Halloween and he'd done really well at the hotel.

Moore also mostly laid down on the couch during his inter-view. Which was a new one. He was friendly enough, but clearly did not give one shit about how Mr. Newspaper Guy perceived him, which I kind of liked. And he was a fantastic conversational-ist. Though, after all that, he did straighten up and put his hat on and made himself presentable for a photo.

So this was a no-brainer. Ten years earlier I probably would've written half the story before I got out of the hotel's parking garage.

Nope. Again, I have no idea why, other than I drank and no longer cared. And no one really seemed to care at work. My daily work, writing the snarky celebrity-ripping People column, was popular with readers. My film reviews were getting done. Sometimes I even waited until after the screening on the way to BART before going to the liquor store (screenings were usually in San Francisco).

Like music criticism, I think I had a semi-knack for movie reviewing. I didn't know as much about film as I did music - and certainly not as much as most real film critics. But my writing made up for it. It sounds cocky, but I could write - at least in newspaper form. It was honestly the only thing I did well, and I won't be Mr. False Modesty by pretending otherwise. But by then, I was pretty terrible at everything else - being a husband, parenting, being a friend. My writing was circling the drain, but I could still do it. A close friend and colleague once told me I was "better at writing shit" than any writer he knew. Which confused me at first until I understood he was complimenting me. I could make something of nothing. Which included writing like I actually knew what the hell I was talking about.

But I'd stopped caring about a lot of things. I stopped entering awards contests - which journalists love and management loves even more, because they think awards make us feel good enough to distract us from all the money we don't make. The only award contest I entered that half-decade was for a freelance column I did for a Bay Area parenting magazine, and the only reason I entered - and won - was that I was still pissed my day job took my newspaper column away. I wanted to win the columnist award, take the stupid thing to my boss and say "Guess who's the best magazine columnist in the Bay Area this year?" And I did.

But I'd stopped trying to get better at my job. I wasn't even ripping off writers I loved anymore. I was once supposed to cover part of San Francisco's huge annual music festival, Outside Lands, during that ugly period. I made it as far as the BART platform. Then I freaked out because I hadn't drank yet that morning, was getting the shakes and anxiety, and knew it would be next to impossible to deal with 100,000 sweaty, inebriated music fans without an accessible, realistic alcohol supply. So I went home, left my boss a message, saying I was sick. Which, technically, wasn't wrong. At least until I got to the liquor store on the way home.

The week Disney unveiled *Rogue One* in 2016 (a few months before I left the paper), I went to a pair of press events - an all day event at Industrial Light and Magic in San Francisco to interview the cast (I got Mads Mikkelsen, which was way better than I thought it would be) and a trip to George Lucas' Skywalker Ranch for food, drinks, and a preview in Lucas's incredible home theater.

Thankfully, there were drinks at the latter, because I started detoxing and feeling like I was going to throw up on a stormtrooper. During the daytime event in San Francisco, thankfully there was a store near the parking garage. Or I wouldn't have lasted inside for five hours (which ended up being amazing for Mr. Star Wars/ Disney freak).

I wasn't a juiced-up, stumbling drunk at work. I just needed the alcohol some days to do my job. I needed it to get back to normal. Which, even I understood, was becoming a huge problem. Even though I was drinking more than a salmon swimming upstream in a raging river, I could still fall back on faking it. Even when I didn't write stories I was supposed to, apparently.

My brain was scattered and as long as I had enough money and opportunity to drink, I didn't really care. And nobody at work said much. Newspapers weren't in a good place and lots of people were trying to figure out how to escape, so maybe they were too busy with their own problems.

Either way, I was coasting on more than a decade of good work. I had two boxes full of awards and people who used to tell me I was great at my job. But not so much those years. I'd been working almost exclusively from home by then, because - frankly - it was easier to drink there, and being around people became uncomfortable, sober or not.

During my lost period - typically 2017 to 2020, though I could argue it started way before then - I had a definite employment problem. I wasn't getting any. I work in a business that basically depends on people talking to people about other people. So it likely was known among other local media people I was an unreliable shithead with a substance problem.

Or maybe I'm just wishing that's true. My work might have deteriorated to the point that no one remembered or cared.

But I did find some non-journalism jobs the ensuing three years. I just couldn't keep them.

There was the job I got at Trader Joe's. I decided my problem wasn't me, it was journalism. I mean, I did it professionally by then for 25 years. But maybe I was wrong. Those middle aged people working at Trader Joe's sure looked happy.

Look at those wild and super fun shirts! And I worked at a grocery store when I was 21 and it wasn't so bad (I absolutely hated it and quit after four months, which felt like four years). Maybe that's where I belonged.

I lasted two days.

Maybe it had something to do with, at the end of my first day, them asking me to restock the liquor department. I'd been sober for at least a few months so, in about 15 minutes, I handled more booze than I had in a long time. All that work obviously made me thirsty.

To qualify, I lasted one day sober. Because, on day two, I decided the only way I was going to get through another day on my feet for eight hours (my feet, legs and back apparently all forgot I wasn't 21 anymore), was with help. And "help" typically meant vodka.

Right. That's some solid long term strategizing, right there. The alcoholic who'd been to rehab I don't know how many times by then would just drink every day for the next 20 years I worked at Trader Joe's. Excellent thinking, as usual. Solid retirement plan.

I got through my second day, with lots of breaks to go to my car, and a lunch break at a nearby liquor store. On the plus side, I felt really friendly that day.

On the down side, I went home, picked a fight with my stepdad over Donald Trump - because that's always a winning, sensible thing to do - and passed out.

I didn't show up for day three.

At least I made it out of the parking lot. A few months earlier, I applied at another Trader Joe's (this was really, somehow, an obvious solution to all my troubles). I showed up for the first interview sober, and did well. They asked me back for a second interview and I somehow accidentally found a really insistent bottle of vodka on the way and had to destroy my day by drinking it before the interview.

I don't remember much, other than it was a short interview. And it was really tiring. I went to my mom's car parked in front of the store and napped for a couple hours, right in the line of sight of the front door, all the employees, and probably the manager who interviewed me. Nevertheless, I persisted ... in sleeping, and didn't get arrested.

I also got a temp agency job, which I actually managed to keep for a few months in 2019. I was stocking shelves in a Nordstrom rack store from 5 a.m. to 1 p.m. or something ridiculous like that. But most of the work was done before the customers showed up and they let us listen to music and I had just rediscovered Jeff Buckley. So ... now I connect one of the greatest artists of my generation to the shoe department at Nordstrom.

But I stayed sober ... until they sent me to the San Francisco store. I drank before I went, made it to my lunch break, then honestly thought no one would notice if I left.

The tremendous amount of insanity I was generating back then is really difficult to fathom at this point in my life.

I made it back to the Pleasant Hill BART station, then passed out in my car until it was dark. I don't remember where I slept that night.

I also worked for Coldwell Banker's big corporate office for a month writing advertising copy. Which I was pretty good at, and they were actually thinking about hiring me permanently. Then something happened - I started getting confident, or settled, or realized I hadn't set fire to my life in a while, so I drank.

After calling in sick for two days, I actually got all the way to the parking garage on day three … only to fall asleep for the rest of the work day. I'm sure my soon-to-be former workmates wondered why the hell I was sleeping in a beat-up Mustang as they walked to their vehicles at the end of the workday.

Well, because that car was really comfortable, for one thing …

At some point that year, I also decided maybe I should go back to journalism and applied for a job at KCBS radio in San Francisco, writing news copy. Which I thought I could still do pretty easily. I could commute, work in the city, and feel like a big time urban journalist, which was the idea way back in 1995 until I met X1 and her daughter and went another direction.

So I went over for an interview with three or four guys and nailed it. Then I went back and actually wrote news for an afternoon. They said it was to see if I could do it and to see if I worked well on deadline, but it might've been to make sure I didn't pass out after sitting in front of a computer for three hours. Like I said, it was the communications industry, and word got around about people. I passed. It was actually kind of fun again.

They called and offered me the job on a Friday. I accepted and said I'd see them on Monday.

Then I decided, since I was making such a grand comeback, I needed to see if I could still drink.

I think that was the weekend I nearly got arrested for moaning … then didn't show up Monday.

I later tried applying again after making up some excuse about having a huge emergency that first week I was not showing up for my new job. The guy who hired me actually laughed when I asked if I could apply again (it was over email, but you could hear the laughter in his email, trust me). I applied again. Shockingly, I never heard back.

For years, my approach to everything involved putting myself in a bad situation with just a sliver of daylight through which to escape. The best-case scenario was simple procrastination and feeling the wonderful rush of getting something done on deadline with milliseconds to spare.

Worst cases usually ranged from being fired or thrown-out of something (friends' homes, cars, jobs, parking lots in which I was trying to sleep) to being near-death.

The day I finally quit the newspaper, I'd just taken a couple weeks off to try outpatient rehab again. It was my last chance and, of course, it worked. For about three days. It sounds like a cop out, but you're not ready until you're ready. And if that means you're not ready when you're about to lose your marriage and your career, then that's what happens. I know; it sounds insane. Because it is.

When I came back to work, I was assigned the last story I wrote for the paper in my 23 years there. A story about the wonders of medical marijuana. Which wasn't necessarily a problem for me, since using marijuana usually meant me rolling up into a ball and finding the nearest corner in which to hide. I hated the stuff. But it still was a drug that sent people to rehab and an editor deciding I should start writing medical marijuana stories - which I was told was the plan moving forward - irritated the hell out of me, since my supervisors knew I just went to rehab.

The day I wrote the story, I had an argument with the editor, who could be testy with me anyway because I'd become such a model employee. But since I was already irritated, things escalated until I finally emailed her (I was working from home) that fine, I'll write the story, and that she could have my resignation when I was done.

I thought she was the problem which, of course, she wasn't. I'd worked for her for about 17 years and, even when I was good at my job, I was still a pain in the ass from time to time. Those past couple years I'd cruised by on past work. She probably enabled me longer than I deserved.

Of course, she announced her retirement the following week. One editor with whom I was friends knew this and was trying to get a hold of me that day to tell me to stop quitting, because my perceived problem - which wasn't really my problem, but I wasn't taking any blame - was about to go away.

Meanwhile, backtracking started on both sides. Human resources got involved. There was talk of taking a leave of absence. I think I started drinking again later that day. I wrote the story. I was told to call human resources back the next day.

Unfortunately, at some point, I reiterated my desire to quit, which I retracted almost immediately. But by then the boss of the boss stationed at the mothership - who didn't care for me and my work - caught wind of what was going on. He sent me a very curt email, saying my resignation was accepted and good luck with the rest of my life.

As I was doing this, my soon-to-be ex-wife - with whom I'd separated a couple weeks earlier - called me out of the blue, saying she'd taken one of our dogs to the vet, the dog had cancer all over her body, and she had to be put down that same day. So I had to gather the kids and bring them to say good-bye, once I was done composing my second fuck-off email.

It was a bad day … a bad month. I was losing important things left and right. But at least I still had alcohol. And I hadn't found my bottom just yet.

Chapter 8

Bottoms Down

The mythological bottom is where these stories either end (death, jail or some other institution) or where the newly redeemed and virtuous storyteller rebounds into triumph, where it's safe to tell the story. Because they pulled themself up safely from a hovel of human animals, the uncleanly borderline insane who are inherently dangerous to normal, non-addicted, law-loving citizens. They've stopped behaving like dirty scavengers and are welcomed back. "Now, that you're back among us, tell your former-and-once-and-again fellows your tales, and spare no tawdry detail, you old scoundrel!"

Well ... if you insist.

We addicts, and the counselors whose salaries depend on us, talk a lot about rock bottom, lowest of the low, that place in darkness where all hope is gone and the worst addicts start trying to make sense of Red Hot Chili Peppers lyrics. Actually, there's no electricity at the bottom unless you can sneak into Starbucks and pretend to be a customer who happens to sit next to a power outlet. Usually the only music is whatever's on repeat inside our unhealthy heads.

Just to be safe, I'll say the jury on my bottom is still out. I still have too many nights feeling lonely or down or I'm eating too much sugar because I'm a diabetic and crave what I can't have (booze, love, rock superstardom), yet my mom keeps sending me and my kids home with big bags of candy, so I ingest too much sugar and wish I was dead.

Not really. But never tell your therapist that (disclaimer: unless, of course, you really mean it).

But my pint … er, point … was that there are still too many nights it's painfully obvious a couple warm gulps of something strong would make it all go away; at least for a while.

But I remember now that means I'd wake up the next morning, go to the liquor store, drink in the parking lot, hate myself, skip work, keep drinking, get fired, hate myself, and do God knows what for the next five days. The last couple times I stayed in my room for hours and watched patterns crawl all over the dry plaster of my wall, even a day after I stopped drinking. I remember once hearing in rehab that alcohol doesn't make you hallucinate. Which, I can assure you, isn't close to true. I must be gifted.

But since it seems mandatory, I do lay claim to a bottom, and it wasn't the last time I drank and forgot to wear pants. Nor was it the five days I spent in the county detox in a junkie barracks with people throwing up all night and a restroom that I still can't think about without gagging.

I think my bottom of bottomy bottoms came over a weekend in January 2019 or 2020. This is how screwed up I was. I'm writing in 2025 and I truly have no idea how one of the most significantly horrible weekends of my life actually happened five or six years ago.

But I remember it was January. And I was wearing shorts, which I only noticed because the temperature was down in the high 30s (I checked when I got home, in case I ever wrote a book).

Not really. But I remember there was a cold spell and the

temperature was in the 30s that week. Which is take-your-shirt-off weather in some places. But I'm from California, the forests and scrub brush of which burn year-round and it only rains when it's time for the mudslides to wash away the burnt timber.

I'm not even sure what day the weekend started - or if it was actually, in fact, a weekend. I've been sorting out those days in my brain for a few years now and have concluded, unless there's terrifying video somewhere, I'll never know.

I do know - speaking of wishing you were dead - I was very depressed and called my high school girlfriend and, somewhere in there, told her I was giving up. That wasn't out of the blue; she and I have been close since we were 15. We periodically saw each other as we got older and proposed marriage to the other at different points of adulthood when the proposer was single, but the proposee happened to be anchored to someone else. So it never quite happened as adults, but we're always more than just close friends. It's weird, but strangely reassuring.

Saying I was giving up that day just meant I was giving up even trying to be sober and was going to take a nap or something. I wasn't able to plan farther. I firmly believe I'm incapable of directly conscious suicide, though there have been a couple times I decided what the hell, I'll just drink myself out of here.

Of course I knew what "giving up" means to most people, and it didn't mean putting a gun to my own head. Too messy and I don't like guns.

Anyway, I must've been convincing, because she called my

mom, who happened to be in the same house as me. Then came yelling and someone decided they couldn't deal with me (again) and called the police. Who had me taken away.

I think it was the third time I'd been taken away while living at that house. Bob called the cops one time, after which I called him a list of unsavory names (Sorry Bob) and another time someone (I don't know who) found me - literally - in a ditch about a quarter mile away, after I walked to the liquor store and, drinking while walking down the street, decided to sit down by a big ditch to rest a second ... then I woke up in the ER.

Big Ditch ... that would be a great alcoholic band name.

This time I do remember. Because I thought - of all the really awful things I'd done to my loved ones - that afternoon was pretty tame. Then again, that's not really for me to say. If I had to deal with me, I would have beat the hell out of me a long time before then.

I felt stupid being hauled away in an ambulance to the county psych ward. I remember thinking "I really hope this isn't the ambulance someone else really needs right now." It was a rare selfless thought ...

This is where the roller coaster gets to the top and starts creeping back down and picking up speed. Things get moving too fast and it's hard to remember every drop and twist when you're done.

The psych ward people let me out after a few hours (I have one brief flash of a memory being there) and, knowing me, I was in such a hurry to power walk to a liquor store, I wasn't about to call the people who just called the cops on me to come get me. So no one knew I wasn't in the county hospital for the entire weekend.

Speaking of the cops, the next thing I remember, I'm in a room with a bunch of other guys. There were no bars (either kind) and there were probably 10 to 15 guys, with a door at each end. I guess the local police had rounded up some drunk-in-public suspects downtown and, since I qualified, off I went. I wasn't scraped up or bruised yet. So there hadn't been a fight.

For some reason, I thought I was in the backroom of a department store. Only with cops in charge.

But something weird was going on. Some of the guys in there started whispering about cops being planted in the room. Or maybe that was me. But I vaguely remember being told by someone in charge that I wouldn't be there long. So I started asking questions and there was more talk about plainclothes cops being in there among us, trying to hear what we were saying.

Naturally, I needed an explanation. So I opened the door - which was unlocked. I think I did this twice. The first time I was told to go back into the room. The second time, before I could ask my question, a couple or three cops were on me immediately, violently slamming me against a wall. I think one used a billy club, judging by the bruises on my chest that lingered the following couple weeks.

The bruises were indisputable, as I later showed witnesses who still assure me I wasn't imagining them. It happened and I remember, as an unexpected burst of violence has a way of clearing your brain for a few minutes.

But I'd also entered a weird phase of my bottom weekend. Indeed, a weird, unique phase in all my years of alcoholism. I wasn't just blacking out; my reality itself was warping. I was paranoid. I thought there were informers, informing what I have no idea. The door was unlocked and I did get roughed up - that I know. I thought it was a set-up. But the next couple days and/or nights became a revolving door of reality snapshots mixed into nightmares mixed into memories I still can't completely differentiate which was which.

I also heard my name from behind the main desk. This was the same police department that employed the cop who was close friends with the separated husband of the person I was seeing on and off (definitely off at this point - golden retrievers wouldn't talk to me during that spell, so I was definitely off-limits to intelligent human women).

I vaguely remember being released the next morning - I don't think I slept, which hardly mattered anymore. I remember a bit more and I also thought I saw a guy who was in the tank with me walking around talking to the other cops, thus reinforcing my undercover-cop-among-us theory.

I spent the next day (after finding a liquor store) walking around town in a surreal haze. My phone was nearly dead and I wandered like a homeless guy (probably because, technically, I was). This downtown was a place where I occasionally worked as a reporter years before, back when I still took showers. It was the town my grandfather's family moved to from Montana during World War II. I'd covered a few court cases there years before, and now it looked like I was about to get a case of my own. So I was very familiar with the landscape. But not from this view. I just walked. I didn't eat. I was constantly looking for cops of which, as the county seat - with courts, the sheriff's office, county jail, and county hospital - there was no shortage.

I'd already been to the hospital and jail. The courthouse came later.

Eventually the low phone charge became an issue, and I wandered into an old union building and mumbled something about being a former member who needed to charge his phone (I actually was a member during the miserable few months I talked about the weather with customers eight hours a day as a 21-year-old Safeway bagger). I tried plugging in my phone, then heard a couple people talking about the guy who wandered and seemed drunk. I looked around and, upon seeing no other wandering drunk guys, realized they meant me and got out of there quickly. I was out of my head, but I knew not to get arrested twice the same weekend.

The previous night in jail - or the department store run by cops, whatever that room was - still freshly occupied my brain, of course. And not just from the pulsating purple bruises on my chest. Very honestly, I was terrified. I thought every police car was full of baton-twirling cops, looking for me. I spent so much energy watching, and dodging, and going between buildings, and up and down hills, and trying to avoid the people who'd arrested me once already. I was exhausted. I couldn't imagine doing that every day. People have no idea how many calories homeless people burn trying to look like they're not doing something deserving arrest.

At some point after the sun went down I found a small neighborhood park. My phone wasn't completely dead, and I'd walked something like 14 miles that day, according to my little app that records such things. The app pretends it's beneficial exercise, but at no millisecond did I look at the bright side and take pride in all the steps I was accumulating like I was a suburban mom escaping for a few hours while the toddler was at daycare. I was physically beat, never mind my mental condition (breaking dawn of insanity). My heart was racing. I'd frightened a dentist a couple years before - when I was fully in my addiction, just before my marriage exploded like an old nuke at the Nevada Test Site - when I showed up with a blood pressure in the 180s and they didn't want to work on me.

I can only assume during my lost weekend my normally-high blood pressure and diabetes were going haywire. My weight was down because I barely ate anymore - at some point around that time I weighed myself at 178, which was 40-45 pounds fewer pounds than two years earlier and 66 pounds less than 2004 or so, when I ate pasta nightly and believed I'd forever be married to a broke yoga teacher. I'd last weighed 178 the year after I graduated from high school. I'd gone from a 36-to-38-inch waist to a loose 32 and had to cut new holes to fasten my shorts.

I was so tired. I felt like I'd been tired for years. So I laid down on a park bench.

The next few hours spent inside my own brain were some of the craziest of my life. When I was in the hospital in 2017 for six days, they had me on a combination of drugs that my lady BFF said had me seeing mice on top of the television in my hospital room. Which I don't remember, but was told, at the very least, they were friendly. There are so many drugs floating about to treat addicts in rehab or the hospital, and a lot of what you end up taking is hit-and-miss, depending on your reaction and what your brain is already going through from all the substance abuse. It's shoot first and adjust to the misses as they go in those places. Eventually they'll find the right drug and dose.

In either a hospital or a rehab, I once dreamed about dark globs with eyes creeping out from under the furniture, trying to kill me. When I woke up, the dark globs were *still* under the chair in my room, and still coming for me. Eventually, as I shook my head clear, they finally vanished. But the line between nightmare and hallucination evaporated for a few seconds, which felt like the longest few seconds of my life. It was terrifying, like something out of a John Carpenter movie. Needless to say, that was the last time I took that particular medication. I was still a year or two away from conscious hallucinations when drinking (and for a day or two after), the duration and intensity of which just get longer and more believable as I age.

But my sleep on the bench that night wasn't fueled by prescription drugs mixing with damaged brain chemistry. That night, it was just my brain on no sleep, no food, way too much alcohol for way too long, and an underweight body whose defenses were shot.

I was a mess.

I laid down and dozed, and got up and walked around, and went back and dozed, and kept repeating the cycle for what felt like hours, but could've been just a few minutes. It's like I was losing my grasp on time and direction. Right - like being in IKEA. Only worse.

During what I thought was one of the times I got up to walk, I thought I found my cousin's house in the dark. He's actually my third cousin - or cousin thrice removed, or however they measure such things. His mom and my mom are first cousins and somehow, even though we were only a few years apart and grew up in the same county, I'd only physically met him the previous year. But we'd hit it off and became friends.

And there was his "house," almost like a weird, low-slung log cabin. The sign on the front said it was some sort of sex house and there was a party going on and people should come through the side gate. There was no door, which I guess is a thing with modern orgy-houses. So I walked the other direction and across the poorly-lit street.

Apparently, I'd found the bad part of town. There was some sort of big wall perpendicular to the street and a store on the other side was being robbed. Then two groups in and out of cars were shooting at each other. So I threw myself against the wall and down on the ground, which was covered in broken glass. It was cutting

the hell out of my face and bare chest (I guess my shirt evaporated?), which was better than being shot. When things cleared up,
I hightailed back to the park and went back to sleep.

I woke up feeling cut up and bruised, from where I hit the
ground and crawled to safety through broken glass.

I initially, and very honestly, believed it really happened. I
didn't feel like I had much time for analysis, because I suddenly
felt an urgency to get indoors and charge my then-dead phone.
When Bottom Weekend was over, I didn't talk about that strange
episode, or even think about it. I just assumed it happened. It was
weeks before I tried processing the evening and concluded it had to
be a nightmare. But that's how damaged my thinking was. At that
degree of alcoholism, even with the alcohol out of one's system,
there's still enough lingering damage to make your brain still live
in a half-drunk fantasy world. It's basically under the impression
it's still drunk and very unhappy about it. It sometimes took weeks
to sort out what was real and what was just terrifying and humiliating fits of imagination.

I also somehow thought the girl that got away knew I was
homeless and just didn't care enough to come get me off the street.
Which was breaking my heart on top of everything else and absolutely ridiculous. No one knew where I was. My mom later said she
thought I was in the hospital all weekend, or she said she would've
looked for me. She was very upset when I told her the story. Which
was my doing, of course. She and Bob should've never been in that
position to have to call for help in evicting me.

I eventually got off the bench, accidentally found the county hospital, and talked a security guard in the lobby into letting me charge my phone enough to call my lifesaver of a friend, Clifton, who picked me up as the sun came up. He wisely refused my request to stop at the liquor store and took me back to my mom's.

By then I must've looked like something emerging from a bombing. I was dirty and limping and slightly stooped (stupid?) over, because my lower back was cramping and my legs were horribly sore. I had some mild frostbite on my right foot - my doctor told me a few weeks later - the two smallest toes had sort of frozen together and the nails were compressed into the skin where I couldn't cut my pinky toenail for about six months. By then it was like a tightly-rolled dead shellfish. I kept thinking I needed the woman who fixed Jim Carey's toes with the explosive electric sander in *Dumb and Dumber*. It took my foot about a year to look human again. It's fine now, but I was kind of worried for a while.

My liver was probably ready to explode, my blood pressure was probably pushing whatever was flowing through my veins like a summer water slide, and my diabetes was leaving enough unfiltered sugar in my body to have me peeing every couple hours at night. Plus there was my nasty-looking softball-sized bruise on my chest, care of law enforcement. But all I could think about was: Am I going to have to wear a sock to bed for the rest of my life so no woman sees that toe and refuses to sleep with me again?

I should put that last paragraph into my online dating profile and watch the ladies start lining up

Luckily, it's normal now - my toes and everything else. It's funny what happens when you stop drinking five meals a day. The blood pressure goes back to normal, the diabetes takes a figurative valium, and the liver pain stops doubling me over every so often, just for fun and to remind me I'm killing myself.

Freezing cold and walking non-stop wasn't exactly healthy exercise. I don't know how homeless people who are actually that way for years survive and manage to keep moving. I wasn't ready for a mere weekend of it and it felt slightly worse than being sucker punched repeatedly all over my body.

I told the story and my mom and Bob let me stay, and I managed to stay sober for a good six months.

But since we're telling tales, when it came to a close second, the junkie barracks in the county detox was right there as my next to bottomy bottom runner-up. If there's anything I'd use to deter people from doing the stupid things I did, there's no better place than the county detox. Where there's no medical supervision for people detoxing, which can kill people. It's basically a place to hold you while you whimper and throw up for five days.

After one of my trips to the hospital - I couldn't say which one chronologically because I just stopped counting - the hospital said they were taking me somewhere to straighten up for five days. Swell, I said, Fine … whatever you say. They were obviously tired of seeing me, and I was more than sick of seeing them.

They had a guy drive me at night in the direction of Concord. I wasn't sure - I was still out of it. They checked me in and immediately put me in a long, darkened room, first bed on the left. The lights were out, but a dull orange street light shone in through the upper windows, lighting the top of the far wall.

Then I noticed the frosty room was full of people trying to sleep and failing miserably. Like the moaning of overacting extras in a zombie movie miserable. I couldn't tell how close or how many, but there were some unhappy addicts trying to detox in that half-dark, half forest fire orange room. It was cold - it was December, I remember that - and I didn't know where I was.

I think it was safe to say I had completely lost control of my life by that point. I gave up trying to figure out where I was and tried to sleep because I had no choice. There was no cable.

The five December days I spent with an unheated room full of sweating, shaking, moaning all-night, barely-responsive addicts was especially bad. When I woke up after the first night, I knew I was sent there from the hospital, but had no idea how I got there, and had no idea where I was. To say I woke up would be to assume I had real sleep, which I didn't. I finally saw my roommates. It wasn't conducive to good sleep hygiene. It didn't seem very enjoyable for them, either.

I sort of regained consciousness and looked out the window at some sort of business park. And I heard a freeway, so I guessed I was north of Highway 4 - near the homeless shelter I was in a couple months earlier. Turned out, I was really four or five miles from Highway 4 and next to a completely different freeway. I didn't figure out exactly where I was for 24 hours, which was a bit disorienting, since I've always been convinced I have a special gift of natural geo-radar, that always worked when I wasn't at IKEA.

I woke up and stumbled out of the barracks into a small, cold lobby. Without thinking, I walked out the front door. There were a few guys loitering out front, smoking and looking like day laborers (later I discovered the detox had its own wing for Spanish speakers, where I accidentally and now hilariously attended my first, and only, non-English AA meeting).

By that point, some of my typical alcoholic fuck-you-ness had returned. I was in no mood for anyone telling me what I could and couldn't do - especially when I hadn't had a drink in 16 hours (enough time to have the alcohol leave your body to start the detox process - shakes, nausea, dry heaving, headache and extreme grumpiness). It was time to find a store and get back to surviving and making a plan. I picked a direction and started walking down the street, getting about a half mile before remembering business parks don't have liquor stores. I stood there for a second, teeth chattering, as the sun finally split the eastern hills.

I had nowhere to go. I didn't even know where I was. I knew I walked down one street, so if I reversed field, I could probably get back where I started.

What the hell else was I going to do? I was a 51-year-old man who didn't even know where he was.

So I went back, where it was explained to me I couldn't leave the premises or they'd call the police. It wasn't a psych hold, because it wasn't a psych facility. I was pretty sure I could leave if

I really wanted to, but at that point I didn't even know where I was, or where I'd go if I could. So I stayed for five days.

I had no idea places like this existed. This county detox wasn't rehab. It wasn't a medical facility and didn't have doctors or nurses, Which is now completely insane to me, since all these rehabs I'd gone to over the years make a huge point of saying we could have seizures and die detoxing.

I mean, they basically said you could die if you simply didn't do what they said all the time. I'd seen people detoxing; I'd seen me detoxing, which was a degrading, helpless and awful feeling. Shaking until your teeth rattle and having no warning before bodily time bombs go off is not a great builder of hopeful self esteem.

But what I saw those five days was a whole new level. People getting sick while not moving in bed - and no one coming to help them. It reminded me of LA during the Rodney King riots, when I drove home from Santa Monica to Hollywood at curfew with entire blocks burning with no firefighters, or traffic, anywhere in sight. Typically when someone screams in their sleep in an official facility, you would expect professional intervention. Grow men crying at either end of the room. I can't even describe the communal bathroom - and I was briefly an elementary school janitor in my early 20s.

There was nothing restful about that restroom. Human waste of every kind, everywhere, and literally millions of insects enjoying it as much as I loathed it. Millions. No one attempted to clean the place the five days I was there.

Just for fun, know that Contra Costa County is one of the

wealthiest counties in California, overall. But perhaps not for uninsured drunks and addicts in 2018.

Then again … what did I expect? This was rock bottom, at least I thought it was. It wasn't yet, but it was close. There's nothing nice about this phase of addiction, especially when it's so bad to cause the system to give up and toss you into a detox with no medical supervision, because the doctors and nurses are other places, treating people they still believe can be helped.

Which isn't to say there weren't some people working there who at least tried. I made friends with the woman at the front desk, who was in charge of giving us meds prescribed elsewhere and helping us find a place to go when our five days were up. Things were so bad for me, I actually tried to get her to let me stay another five.

Hospitals have no patience for people suffering from alcohol poisoning; you spend a lot of time on gurneys in hallways, because the real sick people get rooms. During some of my more lucid moments, I've heard doctors and nurses saying things about "just some drunk" in the hallway. That alcoholism is a disease is a given in rehab, even with the doctors and nurses, so you think they all know that. They don't. Neither do the paramedics, one of whom once belittled me for collapsing when I tried walking.

I really hated myself at that point, as there was nothing I could say or do to defend myself.

But I'm here now. So it got better.

I remember that place and my lost weekend for good reasons.

I don't want to do it again. And, cliche as it sounds, it reminds me sometimes that I'm strong enough to beat this powerful and ugly creature still sleeping somewhere inside me.

I don't say this for sympathy. But as insane as it sounds, some days drinking really feels like a great idea. It still sometimes sounds like a good answer and an old friend. At times it felt as necessary as getting enough air to breathe. And not having it felt like suffocating. It brought panic. It prompted me to do things like steal money from my kids or steal the booze itself from the store when I couldn't steal anyone else's money. One time I didn't even leave the store before I tore the bottle open and got some down my throat.

For a few weeks in 2023, I dated a girl who lived in Martinez. She lived across the street from a small park. It took until my third visit to realize why it looked familiar. I parked next to it, but didn't go back in. It didn't feel uncomfortable. I might've even been thankful to that place, for giving me somewhere to be instead of jail or the psych ward. I smiled to myself when I figured it out. But I didn't go back in. I was done with it.

Chapter 9

Women and Children Last

Much is said about the effect of alcoholism on children and how, if the cycle isn't broken, children carry the disease into their own adulthood and infect another generation.

No shit.

My newspaper columns frequently focused on my kids, to which they learned early not to pay attention because they're smart. And because they have a father who makes jokes out of everything because he can't always deal with life, so he imagines he's living in a sitcom and everyone he knows is watching.

I suppose I used my kids as props, which sounds pretty cheap and selfish. But lots of parents do it (everybody's doing it!) and would never admit it, even if they know they do. The kids were excuses to go places and write about being a superhuman father in said awesome places, raising my kids in much funner and hilarious ways than everyone else while their mom rolled her eyes and smiled in a TV mom way. Which I guess was a win-win for all of us.

Of course, much of it was horseshit.

Well, sometimes. I can tell you mommy wasn't smiling when daddy was falling asleep before the kids or having mini-bottles of vodka fall out of his pocket at Disneyland.

I always wanted to be a dad and, in the back of my mind, I always knew - at least in my 30s, when I had one stepdaughter and just made my first bio daughter - on some level I was heading to a mighty crash with alcoholism. How did I not understand I couldn't do both? I'm still not sure, though my ego likely had a lot to do with it. The streams didn't really cross and explode until I really started screwing up fatherhood. I just never honestly considered I couldn't be an alcoholic and a good father until it was almost too late to separate the two.

I'd had another stepdaughter with another wife in another decade. The second former stepdaughter and I no longer have a relationship. Which - without getting into details about post-divorce propaganda - I suppose I understand. I had an alcoholic stepfather I punched in the face in a bowling alley once (probably twice) for cheating on my mom when I was 17. Things can be very cut and dried when we're young.

When I confronted him, my stepdad tried to bluff me into backing down by introducing me to the girlfriend I was bad mouthing. So I said hello, called her the most insulting thing I could think of, smacked him, and threw a table down into the bowling area. Then I went home because it was Christmas Eve 1985 and I had some Chess King boxes to open in the morning.

The bowling alley on Christmas Eve story (who bowls on Christmas Eve?) won't propel the weepy chapter in which I try to make sense of the bleach-meets-ammonia-mix of fatherhood and alcoholism. It just illustrates how weird life is when you find yourself in a role you swore you'd never play.

My stepdad wasn't all bad; in fact, if I was being honest, I'd admit most of the time he was pretty good. I now understand the job is difficult. Especially if you're an alcoholic. And like him, I was pretty good to my stepkids most of the time.

Some other times weren't so great. I've apologized to all my kids. Even the one who chooses not to be my kid anymore (we still communicated for a year or two after the divorce and then she suddenly decided I'm a serial killer). I can't go back and undo what I did in front of them. I can just say sorry and not do it anymore. That's all anyone can do (or give them money out of guilt, which I sometimes try).

Three of them still love me, so 75 percent will have to do. Which may sound callous, but you can only apologize so much before moving on and trying to prove the bad behavior is behind us.

I couldn't quit drinking for the sake of my wives and kids. If you can, perhaps you didn't really have a problem - I don't know. I can only speak for me. I can do my best to stay sober for my kids, which is a fuck ton easier than pulling yourself up out of the gutter - sometimes literally - and initially getting sober for them or anyone else.

Many rehab veterans roll their eyes when a person new at this says they want to get sober for their family. They don't eyeroll because it's a bad idea. It's an outstanding idea. Whatever it takes. But it doesn't really work that way. Your love for your children has nothing to do with your love of booze (unless you have really awful kids).

Just kidding. But alcohol doesn't ask for, nor does it accept, apologies. It just moves on to its next victim. Thankfully, daughters do accept apologies, So you hedge your bets, hoping you'll stop while there's still space for apologies.

I felt like there was more to apologize for than my kids did. I dismantled two families. As the years went by, my participation in Christmas waned, until I was hiding behind a locked bedroom door, frantically wrapping presents at 9 a.m. Christmas morning, after I did the stomach acrobatics from the previous night. I think our last Christmas together I may have just given up and told my kids I owed them presents. I may have bought one each, but I certainly wasn't an involved dad by Christmas 2016 - the first year we didn't do a family Christmas card and the tree was up at a 45-degree angle and aimed at the neighbors for a day or two until I gathered the strength to fix it.

When I left my home in early 2017, my then 15-year-old - who finally came to live with good old dad two years earlier - had to move back with her mom when my (second) ex-wife basically told her to leave, like she was a tenant behind on the rent. Of course, the marriage was over and my daughter couldn't stay. But the way she treated my daughter didn't - and still doesn't - thrill me. She likely believed my daughter had it coming because of some bad behavior. I say every 15-year-old could theoretically have it coming and we all would be much better parents if we remembered what 15 felt like.

I tell my daughter - who's a great young woman, but clearly still pissed - my ex did it because she was so angry at me, as if I'm still defending my ex-wife. But it's true. She was pissed at me and took it out on my kid.

But where was I? Living with my mom and a lot of empty

bottles. So my ex-wives talked (shudder) and came up with an exit plan and my daughter went back to her mother in Sacramento. Then a few months later, her mother moved her to Placerville (a town that takes great pride in how many people it hanged in the 19th Century). Which was a lot for my daughter to deal with. Then things got worse. About a year or so later - again - still not great with dates during that time of my life - her mother decided to move to Florida.

Right. She thought it best to move my increasingly cosmopolitan teenager across the U.S. to Clearwater, Florida. Which my daughter hated. So she quit school.

I wasn't very thrilled with my ex-wife's decisions. But after all that, she still wasn't Olivia's worst parent during those years. So I couldn't really complain.

Olivia and I had sporadic contact during that time, as I was also having sporadic contact with reality. I didn't care, and that's a burden I'll carry to the grave, simply because I deserve it. Much of the previous decade was about either getting the alcohol I believed necessary for survival or cleaning up long enough to get my life back in order so I could go back to drinking the alcohol I needed to survive, to fuck it up all over again. And so on …

That's the logic of alcoholism. Which I still don't, and will probably never, understand.

Before Olivia turned 18, her mother paroled her from Florida to live with a friend and her unstable family in Placerville. Which went about as well as you would think. When that went south, she went to live with her maternal grandmother for a year in Vacaville, which was between Placerville and my mom's house, until her grandmother died just as I was getting myself together and she could come back to live with me.

Olivia's older sister - my first stepdaughter - came and lived with them most of that year as well, for which I, and their grandmother, were grateful. My eldest daughter - technically stepdaughter, but my daughter - has put up with me longer than any of them and we still have a relationship. Again … I'm grateful.

The idea of putting alcohol before my children is embarrassing. It still hurts them. It hurts me that it hurts them. It shames me. I had a parent who abandoned me before I was born - not why I drank, as far as I know - and I swore I would never do anything to make my kids feel second to anything.

Then I just didn't make them second to a job, or a woman, or a worthwhile cause, or helping others. I basically told them alcohol is more important than them. Then we'd go out in public and I'd behave as if I'd joined Motley Crue.

I failed nearly everyone around me who ever believed in me, and most of those incinerated bridges have not, and will not, be rebuilt. Why keep putting in the work when a loud-talking drunk of a stumbling moron keeps showing up with his vodka-flamethrowing attitude?

Well … I'm better. For now, anyway.

My kids aren't the only ones who forgive. The rest of my family either forgives a lot or just has selective memory. My grandmother was from the Depression/World War II school of thought in which you clench your jaw, ignore problems and move on. Which she did. Meanwhile, the issues just festered into bitterness and disappointment.

But I suppose if we didn't forgive, we wouldn't have anyone with whom to celebrate our dysfunction during the holidays (which we don't really do anymore - too much holiday alcohol under the bridge).

We were all drinkers. Their drinking is their business. I can't condemn them because I understand. I, too, love drinking. I just can't do it anymore.

Since you asked (you didn't, but alcoholics assume you did) I was born in a Salvation Army shelter for unwed mothers in Oakland where, in 1967, white suburban families with some money frequently sequestered their pre-martial fornicating daughters when things went south.

When my 20-year-old mother disappeared, my grandparents told the rest of the family, and the neighbors, she ran away to Lake Tahoe, got married, and didn't come back. Which of course she eventually did only four months later, with a bouncing bald baby who looked a lot like a Catholic basketball player from Berkeley.

It seems people weren't very good at math in 1967.

I started drinking for attention my first year in high school. I found if you aren't the best-looking, being the loudest covers a lot of ground. Drinking was a great way to nuke inhibitions and acting like John Belushi certainly got me attention. I drank, but didn't really depend so much on alcohol through most of my 20s. When I came back from trying to be a rock star in Los Angeles and thought I was getting all literate in college, I noticed most of my new heroes were writers who drank.

Hey, I thought. I'm really good at that. Maybe I should be one of those drunk writers.

Drinking was a weekends-and-some-weeknights thing until the end of my first marriage, around 2005 or 2006. I was miserable and exhibited lots of behavior leading a smarter man to believe he should get a divorce. But we had a preschool-age little girl and a big house and I kind of liked pretending to be an adult. That's when I noticed I was spending a lot of time in the garage, with a bottle I hid in an old gym bag.

When I split up with X1, I suddenly wasn't seeing my kids and got booted from my new adult tract house (but I just dug a koi pond!) and was even more miserable. Of course, I was dating immediately and was "dating" everything within range. Being a music critic and getting really good free tickets to every concert pulling through the Bay Area didn't suck for a newly single guy.

I finally lied to my ex and tried blaming drinking for our relationship being so rotten when I wasn't actually drinking that much (compared to later). I just missed my kids and my house (and that pond).

But then a funny thing happened, I really did start drinking way too much. That's when the excursions in day drinking launched and, eventually, my first bout of detoxing (Hey Doc, I just noticed I start feeling like roadkill when I don't drink for 12 hours ... is that bad?).

It was. So off I went to out-patient rehab for the first time in 2006. I thought it would convince my then-soon-to-be-ex-wife everything was fine and I just needed a bit of repair. She wasn't convinced. Which was OK, actually (again, there was a lot of "dating" that year and the relationship was doomed way before we called it a ballgame).

The funny thing was, even though I lied to her about how much I'd been drinking to justify a loveless marriage (the idea of lying to convince someone I drank *too much* sounds so strange now), I obviously grew into the role with great enthusiasm.

I still thought I had a handle on it all, though. Maybe, though my grip was slipping. Again, one of the great mindfucks of addiction is how falling so low inflates your ego so high: The self-delusion about always being the smartest person in the room, because your behavior wouldn't have lasted so many years without developing some serious cleverness. At least as far as you're concerned.

You think you're inventing new ways of outsmarting spouses, parents, children, friends, bosses ... anyone who might have a negative reaction to you needing to dump down a water glass of vodka before meaningful human interaction.

Then you get to rehab and ask "What the hell am I doing here with all these losers?"

But they aren't losers. They come in all sizes, colors, ages, and tax brackets. I became friends with a former colonel in the

Pakistan military (I cleverly called him "The Colonel") in rehab. I got to know the chief of staff for a state politician of the opposite party from me. I became acquainted with an old guy teetering on homelessness in San Francisco's Tenderloin. And usually, they're there - initially - because they tell stories similar to mine about their families. It takes a while, but the best analogy they use is the one about the cabin being depressurized in an airplane. You have to put the oxygen mask on yourself before you can put one on your loved ones.

I always laughed to myself, thinking if the plane was going down, I'd be screaming too much and looking for the beverage cart for my last drink - for all the drinks - to even see the oxygen mask. But the point was well made.

The worst days of rehab were the ones that were supposed to be the best - when I wasn't in a stairwell: Weekend visiting days, in rehabs in both Oakland and Scotts Valley, located in the fantastic Santa Cruz Mountains. At least in the mountains we had scenery. My kids came most often to Oakland.

It was so strange. No one knew how to act, no longer being able to step around this giant festering, awful boil of alcoholism like it's an old piece of furniture or rusty bucket in the yard no one wants to remove. So we ignored it for years.

Not when the kids come to visit dad in rehab, which wasn't awkward at all.

"How are you?"

"Fine. Have you grown?"

"No. I'm 27."

"Right. Well ... they give us food here."

"That's nice. So are you learning not to be a volcanic asshole anymore?"

"I hope so. But they don't let us drink."

"That's the point."

"Right. We had breakfast this morning. Hey, look at this plant over here…"

My youngest turned nine, then 10, during two separate stints in rehab. I missed two birthdays in a row because I wasn't fit to be around other humans, and certainly not children. Not even my own children, who were unfortunately used to me. I had to send flowers. Which wasn't exactly the best way to make her feel better.

She knew daddy was sick, and her mother tried to explain to her what an alcoholic is. Actually, she tried explaining it to her when she was six or seven. I know that, because she asked me one afternoon what an "Alkanahaulwack" is. And was I one of them?

I wasn't expecting that. But I knew the term when I was her age, because I heard the word thrown at my grandfather quite frequently.. So, after I asked her where she heard that word, I probably tried to distract her by showing her a plant.

My daughters asking when I was coming home was also pretty brutal. Almost as bad as when they left and everyone was crying, and I wondered how any father could allow this to happen to their children? Everytime they left I felt like I did when I was 8 or 9 and my private school Christmas choir sang at a local department store.

My mom and grandma were there and we were told we could go home with our families afterward.

So I found mine and they said to go tell the headmaster I was leaving. OK, easy enough. I went back through these doors and through a backroom to where kids were getting on the bus by the loading dock. I told the school boss my home boss - my grandmother - said I should let him know I was going home with them.

Well, of course he wasn't going to let a little kid just walk around the store alone, not even in the '70s. This guy was, overall, someone who ruled the school with an iron, Jesus-loving fist. They can hit you at private school - at least back then - and he did, more than once. In first or second grade, he caught me looking into the girls bathroom (I was curious how it was decorated) and took me to the girls lost and found and made me dress up in discarded girl clothes which, come to think of it, might be illegal in some states now. But, on the bright side, probably informed some of my better fashion choices when playing in '80s bands.

Anyway, he wouldn't let me go, escorted me onto the bus so I wouldn't make a run for it, and something inside me snapped. I felt trapped and claustrophobic and abandoned and sick to my stomach. My grandma and mom were waiting for me! Didn't he understand that? I think I had my first ever panic attack - I was numb and couldn't talk. Which now seems ridiculous - I was just going back to school for a couple hours, then back to the same home in which I was bored every afternoon. But it was a terrifying experience that somehow still makes me feel afraid and a bit weak.

I felt the same way when my children left me those few Sunday afternoons. They didn't want to leave and I couldn't go with them. And I couldn't drink the panic and sadness and loss of hope away because I was in a stupid rehab, because I was an alcoholic. A disease of choice - and I made my choice over and over until I was confined to a building in Oakland.

They say you can't get sober for your kids and there's some real truth to that. You have to get yourself together and get your own oxygen mask on first, bleh, bleh ...whatever. But you can stay sober for your kids, and there are plenty of nights when my stomach hurts from thinking about friends I no longer have and people I betrayed and women I loved (well, one) who gave up on me and I begin the old rationalization that a couple drinks won't hurt ... I'll feel better and wake up and start the sobriety clock fresh from zero tomorrow morning.

Then I remember I can't. I now live with two daughters who came and saw me in rehab and saw me at my worst and who I abandoned for a few years (I just looked at a picture of my youngest in a softball uniform, playing for a team I don't remember her playing for. So I'm guessing I missed that season).

But both these girls made a conscious decision to live with me now, instead of their mothers. I did not try convincing either of them, because I know who I am, I know what I am at my worst, and I don't wish that on either of them. I know, no matter what they say, I'm not the world's greatest father. Not when you look at the entire body of work. But they chose - and keep choosing - to believe in me, despite all the years of evidence working against me. That's the loyalty of real love and, in return, they will get all my love and loyalty. Not because I owe them - though I do.

So how do I betray that? The only way is to take a drink and re-light the fuse to my life bomb.

That's not to say I won't someday. But we're taught to do it one day - one hour - one minute - at a time, if necessary. Some nights that has to be enough.

Chapter 10

Get Back

You know what's nice about not drinking anymore? Telling a story and someone not rolling their eyes and cutting you off to say they already heard it, you idiot.

Especially if that someone is one of your children, who curiously stares like maybe you're some sort of sick animal they found in the yard. The look is much different from your wife, conveying enough anger to force you to shrink down and offer a pathetic half-smile in apology for "forgetting." You shrug, smile again, and say "my memory must be going."

Well … it is. But not the way they say it's supposed to go.

Gasoline is burning it from your brain. It's being sucked up, boiling away nutrients and knowledge as the alcohol dehydrates not only your skin, your eyeballs, your brain and body fluid … it changes your nutrient-rich, life-giving deep red blood into something resembling the yellow marsh at the end of the once-mighty Colorado River after civilization sucks it dry.

Of course it takes your memory. It's an invading army of fluid that somehow dries, chaps and drowns cells at the same time, attacking your intellectual fortress and supreme command center: the brain itself. Headquarters - literally, right up there on the quarters of your head - is being parched and sucked dry by a liquid.

Will it be back? Will the muscley recall and magical miles of tiny, perfect electrical connections comprising thoughts and memories and knowledge and facts and reason ever come back?

Beats me.

But that moment you smile and try to joke with your spouse

"my memory must be going," you both understand it really means "I might as well open my head and pour the vodka directly onto my brain, because gulping down booze every time I encounter something resembling an emotion and, in the process, destroying my short term memory to the point of not telling you a stupid story I just told you yesterday, is just about the same thing."

Yeah. Sometimes the stories repeated themselves ... daily. It's an excellent way to get people to stop listening to anything you say.

Cue my big sober reality rebuild which, if this was a movie, would start with the training montage to some upbeat guitar rock over intense singing about beating odds and not throwing up in the front yard.

Mine might look more like Chris Rock's in *New Jack City* than Rocky Balboa flexing and chasing chickens (I always wondered if he ate the chicken once he caught it). For lack of any other ideas, daily exercise was the basis of my comeback. It woke my brain every morning and put me in the right mood, with just the right amount of confidence I'd lacked for years, to finally get back on track.

Don't get me wrong. I didn't become attractive. But my eyes are a bit more focused, my skin is a healthier color, and, best of all, I'm not decomposing in a box. So, in that context, I think I look pretty good.

The real accomplishment is feeling human, without booze, and having a way to clear my brain every morning and get the engine started. I don't run marathons or deadlift 800 pounds. All it takes is even a little bit of effort. Some days it only takes me leaving my house, driving to the gym, riding a stationary bike for 20 minutes, and coming home without endangering myself and others.

Other days, I listen to bad heavy metal and run around the cut-rate gym picking things up until I want to fall over. Which, ironically, is what happened sometimes when I drank. Whatever the approach, I try to do as much as I can, but the important point is getting out of the house and moving. And not talking to anyone, in case I start repeating myself again. It's a process. Good thing direct communication is illegal at gyms. Only quick glances when you think no one's looking.

I don't talk nearly as much anymore. Talking used to get me in as much trouble as the booze that preceded it. Apparently I wasn't as charming, sexy and insightful as I believed.

So even though I'm not drinking, I've cut way down on the talking, just in case I have some sort of weird flashback and start telling someone how good of an athlete I could've been or how my band should've been much bigger.

I keep quiet and go to the gym, where I also keep quiet, lift things until out of breath (not long), and watch people watch other people to see if they're looking at them and, if they are, are they giving away any hints they might be impressed?

I was so used to being red-faced and sweaty from years of shocking my body with water glasses of vodka (amount-wise. I stopped using glasses years ago, as they just added a step to the process), that when I started exercising, no one noticed much of a difference. A couple times I stopped by my mom's house after the gym early in my new routine, and she gave me the "you're drinking again, aren't you?" look.

At the beginning of the century, I weighed 244 pounds and had a size 38 waist. I wasn't as healthy, but I also was more prone to coming down with periodic bouts of being an asshole. Now I hover between 205 and 210 and size 34 pants hang loose from my waist. And, as far as I know, I'm not such an asshole because - maybe - I just understand I no longer have that much leeway. Or maybe studies show that people who don't drink too much on Halloween and chase kids through the neighborhood for taking too much candy makes for a nicer person. Either way, I'll take it. I'm sure my brain looks much nicer - less angry. Less sweaty.

As my periods of sobriety went from 38 days before the next drink, to 60 days before a drink, to 140 days, to …six months, a year … I noticed the more I exercised, the longer I went without booze. Of course, other things helped too, like having a job, which really didn't stick until I got past six months of sobriety. Or not putting myself in bad situations (sleeping on park benches in winter, agreeing to restock the liquor aisle, drinking during treatment, etc.).

Remembering when the real rebuild started is kind of foggy since, like most alcoholics, I've loudly announced my commitment to changing my life for the better approximately 30,000 times over three decades to anyone who will listen. Which is why no one dates me who knew me more than five years ago. I can be sober for two years, fall off the wagon, jump right back on and determinedly say

I'm back and better than ever and yadda yadda. When I see the cats roll their eyes and leave the room, I know everyone's heard enough.

People want proof, which I understand (checks title of book). Math terrifies me, so I hate counting days. But I keep track so I can fling a number back at people when they question me. Though numbers don't always matter when it comes to sobriety. I know people with more than a decade of sobriety who fell hard off the wagon (we must find something better than "the wagon" to fall off. Maybe "the space train"?) and had to start all over. Because when you fall, you usually start drinking again with the same ferocity as the last time, no matter the years in between. Which is problematic for me, as I roll up in a tight ball and do nothing but call Ubers to take me to the liquor store, because someone usually confiscates my keys).

I'm at an age where I no longer mourn my past life. At least as far as going to clubs, bars, orgies at my cousin's house, etc. I've given up on some cities even, which is kind of sad when I think about Las Vegas. Maybe someday. At this point, just landing at the airport in Las Vegas would kill me. I'd step off the plane and just explode, right there on the jetway. I used to love Las Vegas - from what I remember - but can't even think about it anymore. This is no joke - I literally thought of Vegas one night and fell off the wagon. Which just goes to show what a mess I was (or how much fun I don't remember having in Las Vegas).

For a few months during the last half of 2019, I was twisting my almost six-foot body to sleep every night on my friend's four-foot-long sofa under a blanket on a covered patio. Right - like fun size camping. I again made the brutal mistake of wondering about having a real relationship with the girl I'd been sort of seeing for a couple years. She sometimes did work around casinos and I certainly liked the free drinks they serve in casinos.

I got to thinking one night how fun it would be to go to a casino together. Then I started thinking "There's going to be a time she wants to go to a casino and drink some of those free drinks. And if I'm not drinking, then I can't go to a casino and drink the free drinks, which means she might feel like she can't go to a casino and drink free drinks, which isn't fair to her at all, so maybe I'll just drink only in casinos from now on."

I made a tremendous amount of sense in 2019.

So I thought, "Since this girl is what I want, and of course I want to go to casinos with her because she loves casinos and it's not fair for her to not go to casinos, I better see if I can just have one drink and be OK, like I would in a casino.. So I'll just try that - now, here in Concord, CA. - to give it a test run."

Seriously. I said that to me. If you don't believe me, just ask me.

I was very serious. I was crashed on a couch on a patio at the age of 52 - unemployed and driving my mom's 20-year-old car with a hole in its roof because of my inability to have a taste of alcohol without immediately assaulting the nearest liquor cabinet and, eventually, falling over and speaking a new language.

I decided I needed to see if I could just have a couple drinks like a civilized person because I was sure that my future happiness depended on whether I could go to a casino with a woman who wasn't talking to me. Made all the sense in the world.

And surprise … it didn't work very well. I think I was moaning in front of the police 16 hours later.

OK, how did I get here? Thanks for asking.

We covered the bottom analogy, but yes … I hit it hard, like causing the puff of smoke following Wile E. Coyote plunging from a cliff. I did have some help: I got thrown out of my mom and Bob's house for the last time. My daughter's grandmother died the same week and she had nowhere to live. I was really tired of it all - it was the last week of July 2020 when the pandemic was in full kill mode, so it was a surreal time of transition for everyone. I hadn't lived on my own in three-and-a-half years, and that barely counted because, for 10 years, I had a wife who made more money than me and put up with most of my loony behavior..

Everything just came together, which is weird to say about a period when a pandemic was killing millions. Typical bass ackwards approach for me. While everyone freaked out, stayed home, and day drank out of fear, I somehow, mostly, got sober during the pandemic. I'd been sober for six months before my last three-day slip at my mom's house in July 2020. I'd just sort of reconciled with the woman I loved, which meant I had something to smash into pieces again. But my daughter really needed a dad, and I was really tired.. So I stopped drinking and overthinking and started looking for places to live.

The first half dozen potential landing spots turned me down because they required credit checks, and my credit was in smoking ruins from 2017 (I forgot to pay bills, as I was very busy working on my competitive day drinking that year). I got on Craigslist and immediately went to the second place that looked acceptable. It was in Lafayette - an upper income community I didn't include in my first search parameters because I just figured I couldn't afford it and don't eat at many outdoor cafes with a dog in my purse.

Nevertheless, I found a cool little apartment building constructed in the 50s that reminded me of some of the buildings I ran around like a drunk maniac when I lived in Hollywood. There was an L-shaped courtyard half-framing a pool, and all the white steel fencing was outlined in some rust, with big oversized plants lining the borders. This particular unit was tiny, which is why it was affordable. I could manage tiny.

Maybe. I was still pretty terrified. I was almost 53, had owned a couple homes, half-raised some children, and got recognized in front of liquor stores. But I was terrified.

During those last few months at mom's, I worked part-time for a Korean AI in education company at which my punk rock/tech inventor/libertarian friend Rob got me a job.

Rob's a good guy, even though he's wrong about almost everything he says that doesn't involve cars, tech and other things I don't understand. Rob and I became friends during my music writer days, because he was still convinced he was absolutely going to become a rock star in his mid-30s and kept sending me demos and pestering me until I finally broke down and wrote about his band so he would leave me alone.

His band was good, which has nothing to do with getting record deals. But the guy just wouldn't quit, plus he talked really fast, like the fuse on the stick of dynamite was almost burnt down, but he still had something to say before the explosion. Rob would just, out of the blue, start talking about inventing things for the CIA. It was a little nerve wracking. But I checked and found I didn't have any friends even remotely like him, and we got along well, so we became friends. After which he immediately decided I don't value money enough (uh, yeah … *journalism*). So when I needed a job, he got me one.

I made good money for four months, allegedly doing part-time public relations work, but in reality going to a lot of Zoom meetings where Korean-American men younger than me talked about disrupting industries and overseas markets and unicorns and K-pop and the Silicon Valley, but never at any time explaining to me exactly what it was I was supposed to be doing.

I collected a bunch of cash over four months, finally drank and stopped showing up to the Zoom meetings at which no one ever explained to me exactly what we were selling and to whom (I still don't know).

But the money was real and I owe a great debt to my punk rock/ entrepreneur/tech inventor/libertarian friend Rob for getting me a job where no one explained to me what they sold or what I was publicizing or why.

By the way, this is how screwy the Silicon Valley/tech bro world is: Those were the most ridiculous four months of my life and I didn't have a single drop of alcohol the entire time. And it was still weirder than sleeping on a park bench and dreaming about my third cousin not letting me into his orgy. But the checks didn't bounce, so I kept smiling at the bad jokes and nodded and said things like "Yes, let's disrupt that process and expand those disrupting overseas markets with unicorns and speculate some things and stuff."

They also talked a lot about ice cream. Every other meeting there was a get-to-know-you exercise in which we all told the other 10-12 people on the call from around the world our favorite ice cream. Then someone would start talking about how the mythical head of the company was going to fly us all to South Korea so we could go get drunk in a Karaoke bar and disrupt some ice cream or something.

Because none of that is ridiculous enough, know that the company, which started in Korea, had the same name as an over-the-counter medication here in the U.S. that treats lice and crabs. Seriously. Every time they said the name, I had a flashback to getting bugs from a radio DJ girl with a purple Mohawk when I lived in L.A. (they're gone now). At one point, I tried explaining this to one of the guys and asked, only half-jokingly, if they really wanted Americans to think about having crabs and head lice every time someone said the company's name out loud. To which he laughed and asked what my favorite ice cream was.

I honestly don't know how all these Silicon Valley people supposedly make billions of dollars. I saw the allure that pulled so many of my newspaper colleagues into PR over the years - easy money! Yay! They don't pay us with used vegetables!

But, my God, it was boring. And it was all bullshit. I mean, I'll sit on Zoom and talk about disrupting Korean ice cream all you want if you're paying me enough - and they were. But after four months, I just couldn't take it anymore. Which might've been why I got mad and drank. I'm not exactly sure what happened that time. Though, if I remember correctly, I was starting to buy into all the legal cannabis talk and, conveniently forgetting how any sort of marijuana use over the years usually left me tightly rolled up like human sushi in a paranoid flesh ball in the corner of a room, praying no one would ask me what my favorite ice cream was.

So I ordered some cannabis oil - with THC, the active psychoactive ingredient, which you don't have to ingest if you just want whatever health benefits you believe cannabis brings. But, of course, the addict needed to try the THC-soaked oil, because even if you're supposed to be sober, how can you turn down the possibility of leaving reality for a bit? I had a terrible night. Couldn't sleep, felt like my head weighed a couple hundred pounds, hallucinated a little, and couldn't wait for the effect to go away.

Then the next day I did what I always did since I was 17 years old if I took drugs I didn't like. I drank them out of my system. So I bought some vodka. Which did the trick for the next three or four days and got me kicked out of the house right before I moved anyway. You can't fire me; I quit!

But when that wore off, I had some money in the bank and was ready to roll. But I started freaking out. I didn't know if I was ready. I'd been protected by my parents, my sponsor, some new AA friends, some rehab counselors, when I was either rolled up into a drunken ball or trying to stay sober while still ignoring the real world for the past three-and-a-half years. I was genuinely scared I couldn't live on my own, forget taking care of my daughter. The more I thought about it and considered all the things that could go wrong - and there were a lot - the more paralyzed I became.

At a loss over what to do, I went back to the same approach I used everytime I made a serious progression in my life. I asked what was the worst that could happen, acknowledged that, yes, it could be death, but that was certainly something I hadn't tried yet. I totally gave in, absolutely shut down all brain speculation, figuratively shut my eyes, and just did it.

Right. Nike swoosh. Just do it, baby. And it worked, for the most part. So far.

There were some bumps in the road the next year, to be sure. Olivia was 18. The last time we lived together she'd just turned 15, which is only three-and-a-half years in real time, but a lot of things about my little girl had changed. She'd been through a bad spell as well - moved four or five times, once to an insane third-world dictatorial religious habitat across the U.S. called Florida, then set free at 17 to come back across the country and live with a friend, which was almost as good an idea as me deciding to test drink because I thought I'd be forced into a casino someday.

We bumped heads a bit at first until I realized I had to let go of some control. She was, technically, an adult; she'd changed, and I didn't really know if I had the moral high ground to act like her father again. So I went slow. I learned how to bite my lip, let her make her mistakes and experience growing pains as I did the same at 53 years old.

I also had another daughter back in my life regularly. Lucy was 13 and we hadn't seen much of each other. I also went slow in that regard. It wasn't easy. Her mother was in a firm relationship with SB, which was fine by me; I expected her to be with a new man immediately after our split, just not that one. He fulfilled my every expectation of his step-parenting abilities the next three years. But I couldn't say much at the time, as I was off attacking liquor stores, escaping rehab and sleeping in a car.

But at least I wasn't cruel to animals or fixated on dog shit.

They bought some property and chickens and dogs and were trying to live their American dream, which apparently entailed treating my daughter like she was to be seen and not heard. There were a few things about which my daughter told me that made me want to attack someone with a harpoon.

I'll keep most of those tales to myself, except the decision that broke the alcoholic camel's back. While my daughter was out at a nice restaurant in San Francisco with my mom and me, he repeatedly texted her, apparently dumbfounded as to why she couldn't come right home and clean up after his dog pack. As punishment for having a nice night out at the theater with her grandmother, there was a bag of dogshit in her bed when she got home.

She was officially living with me an hour later.

I stayed sober and didn't harpoon anyone. But the incident - which is a really nice way of putting it - did motivate me to move to a bigger house and bring my daughter to live with me, so she didn't have flashbacks every time she got into bed, I also didn't want my animal-loving, sensitive child to have to witness the next time he was less than polite to an animal (not telling those stories because why ruin our fun?). All's well that ends with my daughter getting into a shit-free bed every night now.

I was two years and three months sober and sailing along like I just might make it. Of course, when you've been sober that long - something that honestly seemed impossible a few years ago - something else unexpected is sneaking up on you: Yourself.

Chapter 11

Didn't See That Coming

Meat was stuck to my sock.

It was early 2024 and I was willingly on the floor (this time), because I decided to remember I had a body and it probably needed waking up, since it did slightly less than a corpse the previous week.

I decided to try remembering what my legs felt like with a very pedestrian and tentative leg stretch. Nothing complicated. I wasn't trying to impress someone with my yoga skills, of which I had none. I was less flexible than my daughter's very friendly, 583-pound cat, which sat with its big hairy belly rolling toward me, watching with mild interest.

Come to think of it … he might be a small cow.

I looked down at my foot and there it was. A hunk of meat. A small one, to be sure. But meat nonetheless. Maybe cubed, possibly cooked. Definitely processed. Not mine, as in, not from my body. It looked too bright and healthy … dead, but ironically definitely a healthier shade than me.

I vaguely recalled a pizza box from the previous night; OK … pizza meat, I guessed.

It was about a week after I woke up one morning, looked down at the side of my bed, saw an unopened White Claw I'd swiped from my daughter's 22nd birthday party the night before, and decided to pop it open without a shred of thought as to the consequences.

A morning drink. My arch nemesis for years. My killer of dreams. The rock heaved through the illusionary plate glass window through which I somehow saw myself drinking like a normal person again.

White Claw. Right. I was destroyed by the starter drink of 15-year-old suburban girls.. The hard-drinking writer who, in his younger days, saw himself concocting romantic tales of non-fiction, death-defying, high adventure while slugging bourbon like his heroes. And, like them, always landing back on his feet to start the next adventure, chapter and bottle (never mind how many of them blew their own heads off).

I was in my 57th year of life and trying to choke down a White Claw - essentially this generation's California Cooler - on a bright East Bay Area weekend morning.

"Choking" actually isn't the right word. Those things go down slightly smoother than air. I think kids now chase scary tap water with White Claw.

Seriously, kids are terrified of tap water now. They drink those God-awful burnt cinnamon shot things from 7-11 and smoke candy tobacco and pot ten times stronger than it used to be and eat pills the source of which they have no inkling. But tap water? It's like asking them to drink directly from a marsh.

Now get off my damn lawn.

Nevertheless, the White Claw contained alcohol and I knew it. And wanted it - me, Mr. "I'm so secure in my sobriety I'm writing a book and admitting some horrible shit that almost killed me."

Everyone illustrates their miraculous brushes with death saying things like "The doctor said one more millimeter ... another five minutes ... had I not been wearing my George Costanza wallet in my front shirt pocket and I would've died, etc."

Really, there were more than a few times.

But as far as writing a book, I felt like two years of the straight and narrow though sometimes wobbly was enough time to turn around and talk like an expert recovered sober person which, of course, I never was. Most aren't, but going to enough AA meetings teaches you the jargon and makes you feel like you belong. You're in recovery. It's another one of those cliches with which they club you in rehab. You're not a former alcoholic. You're not even a recovered alcoholic. You're a *recovering* alcoholic.

Well. I. Fucking. Guess. They. Were. Right, weren't they? Because I had a piece of meat on my foot and was laying on the floor, *recovering* from a bad week that started with a *fucking White Claw*.

This time seemingly broke the now-predictable pattern of the hole getting a bit deeper every time I drink and grab my shovel. I managed to keep my job and not totally destroy my life. I also managed to contain the animal behavior to non-work hours. But I'm not a frat kid. When I drink, I get serious.

So, in theory, I just got to work like I had to get the drinking done, which makes absolutely no sense, but none of it does. I won't say it's a skill, because that's insulting to all the people who have died from this thing.

But suddenly there's no food in the house, which you don't need anyway, because you stopped eating days ago. The garbage doesn't get taken out. If it gets really bad, you have wounds you don't remember getting. Maybe hard-to-scrub-off tape marks on your arm from the IV that usually takes five days to vanish, which indicates someone took you to the hospital. You did manage to hold off day-drinking this time until your days off, but immediately went so overboard that you (me) needed six-to-eight hours of medical intervention.

What's worse is that your kids have to witness at least part of it. They have to call one of your two designated sober buddies to come help. Later there might be a missing patch of skin appearing between your eye and ear. It's the size of a tennis ball and looks inexplicably like someone took a cheese grater to your face. It probably looks that way because, and this is speculation, you fell against the wall outside your house and literally grated your own face. It looks like a little boy's knee when he falls off his bike on a serrated driveway.

When you finally stop drinking, and you're done with the usual detox period, you emerge from the vampire cave to risk mingling with humans again. The damaged face skin starts scabbing and peeling away - terribly fun to watch strangers with whom you converse work so hard to not look at your face while they clearly wonder what in God's name this grown man has been doing.

The buddy who comes to help was the friend for whom you performed the same service last year. You've danced this dance before; the only thing that changes is who leads. It's quite possible this is getting really old, and there's some rage involved. You don't want your kids to have names of people to call to come help them when you drink too much and may need medical attention. How do you explain that later?

Honesty helps. And is really the only way. Because these kids aren't stupid, and you're sick of lying.

Just as your buddy hit you a few times last year when he was drinking and required help (luckily he's smaller than you and can't really hurt you if you see it coming). It's also quite possible you remembered that and tried to hit him with a guitar. Which is still speculation (you don't remember, but ... witnesses). It's very possible you've watched the old video of Keith Richards hitting that fan with his guitar on the Rolling Stones 1981 tour a few too many times.

Speaking of Richards - a role model to so many addict musicians despite being a physical freak who logically should've died decades ago - there's nothing romantic or glamorous about frightening one's children or only being able to express one's emotions through substance abuse. This I know, the hard way.

Richards has been, and always will be, one of my heroes. I met him once for about nine seconds which, up until then, may have been the greatest nine seconds of my life. I love his music and I love his attitude, still. There's no one like him.

But that's just it. There's one Keith Richards. The rest of us will die trying. Many have.

I admit my addicted musical, literary and film heroes' mere continued existence fueled much of my early use. Not their fault - my choice. But so many budding musicians, actors and writers, among so many other types of creators, try portraying substance abuse as being part of the job. I know I did, which was little more than an excuse.

Good art and substance abuse are more frequently mutually exclusive as not. They can feed each other, but only for so long. Which is why we get so many artists, musicians and writers dying young from substance abuse. Some use chemicals to deal with the noise in their brain, but that's frequently no different than construction workers or real estate agents or anyone else. We feed a bullshit idea of doing your best work and dying young and leaving a good-looking corpse, as if getting old would lessen the work's value.

Go find Kurt Cobain's death photos on the Internet and tell me what's romantic. That's hardcore depression. He would've likely been a drug addict whether he was a musician or not.

Charles Bukowski and Richards - two of my favorites - could've been just as good without the substances, but the chemicals became part of their work. They're the honest ones who are open about their use that make it seem romantic. It's not a requirement of the job. Though it became almost all of Bukowski's public identity. He still would've been an exceptional writer without it. He just would've had to find a different gimmick.

In most cases, weirdo artists are weirdo artists, with or without substances. I won't lie - I used drugs and alcohol when doing some good work. But I was also young and enthusiastic and life felt fresh. The using just isn't sustainable. You might argue it's sustainable for

80-something Richards, but the Stones haven't done great work since the 1970s and he's been off heroin for decades. He's just managed to somehow stay alive.

Eventually, inevitably, and almost always, the substance becomes a liability to creation, because our brains just weren't built for this.

A big part of my problem has been subscribing to the illusion. I now know I do better work without it, and always have. Alcoholism is in my genes, in both my biological families. I believe that, genetically, something sits there, waiting to be activated. Some people in my collective family are not addicts, because they didn't pull the lever, and maybe it just skipped them. But I did enough for all of us.

I still occasionally struggle with things like boredom, which can be remedied by those willing to push themselves to find a way to create through it. Anxiety and pain are the other two reasons I want to use. I went to court recently to redo my child custody agreement and child support. I finally have some legal standing with my 16-year-old for the first time in seven years. She feels like I'm her dad again, which feels wonderful.

I still want to dull the anxiety and depression. Welcome to Earth 2025. There are ways to push through, because I have to. I've done so much damage to myself - it's not irreparable, but I have to be creative and find ways through with things like exercise, reading, movies, trying to get involved with my kids (sometimes failing, but trying is key). I used to meditate, but seem to struggle with that now. Perhaps, as with everything else, I should keep trying.

Because the second I take a drink, there's a good chance I've just destroyed weeks that haven't happened yet. Even if I can manage work in between drinking episodes, it's not exactly my best. I went through a phase where I simply plunged off the cliff into the speeding binge river and stopped working altogether, because I'm trying not to drown. Then if I stopped after a week - no promises - It took another week to recover. One drink and I can easily burn a month of my life. One of these times, if I keep trying, I won't come back.

I turn 58 this year. My dad died at 61. I have no idea how much life I have left and I don't want to shorten it more than I already have. While not much of a father to me, my dad showed every sign of being an exceptional grandfather. But he didn't take care of himself - to be fair, he had a medical condition that probably could've been managed. But he also lived his own way and was going to do what he was going to do. He died before he could meet his youngest daughter, who was adopted, and her two kids, or my youngest daughter.

It makes me sad. But it's also hypocritical for me to say I couldn't easily do the same thing and die before I meet my grand-kids. And that's not fair to them. It's not right.

Maybe that's why I'm going public - enough people knowing forces me to move forward.

Then again, most everyone connected to me already knows to different degrees. Like I said, I've taken a flamethrower to so many bridges, I'm all out of kerosene.

Before my last speed bump, I felt I had my shit together enough to look back and discuss alcoholism with authority, like I was lying to Oprah or public speaking or doing a book tour. A retrospective, like getting clear of the firestorm, taking a breath, and telling the story from safe ground. But there is no safe ground, which I knew in my brain, but the news didn't reach my ego..

Does that make any sense?

None of this does. I thought I had enough authority to write a book about this cycle (wash, rinse, drink, vomit, sleep, repeat) because the plane had crashed and I jumped free. Then just as I was patting myself on the back and marveling at the wreckage I escaped, I didn't notice the next one coming in for a crash landing.

It's like Gandalf in *The Lord of the Rings*, dispatching the Balrog into the void and turning around and taking a deep victory breath … just before Mr. Balrog flings his fire-whip back around to pull Gandalf down into the darkness with him. Then you (alcoholic Gandalf) fight all the way down, everyone thinks you should be dead and stops inviting you to their holiday parties, only to have you show up seemingly years later in a clean new robe, not really knowing who you are anymore.

There's always another plane or Balrog coming. So, like I tell my kids so they don't get accosted on public transportation (I've bought them weapons) be aware of your surroundings.

I stopped being aware of my surroundings and forgot it was 2024, not 2014. Or 1994. Or 1984.

But I've come too far to stop now.

Relapse is part of recovery. It happens. Just don't relapse yourself to death. Beating yourself up is way too easy. What are you going to do now ... quit trying?

In times like these, when you're desperate for something to make sense, to which you can hold on, I happened to read something saying you can't define yourself by your failure. Be honest, but have some self-compassion. It's the only way to move on.

Author and researcher Brene Brown addressed what it means to be strong, which I saw while looking for some strength: "The core of mental toughness is actually self-compassion. People who are mentally tough stay mentally tough because they don't slip easily into shame or self-criticism or self-loathing."

Well ... it was a bit late for that, wasn't it? But point taken. Who wants to waste time feeling sorry for oneself? I'm a grown man who's been to rehab 10 or 11 times, as far as I know. I'm the only one responsible for my behavior. I can't change what I did. So I apologized - again - and carefully moved forward, hoping that's enough for the people I love most who, coincidentally, I always hurt the most.

And because I'm an alcoholic (liar), I struggled the first couple days of this latest wagon tumble with the idea of lying about it. Let's pretend it didn't happen and finish the original plan, if I actually had a plan.

The ensuing couple weeks was the towel snap to the nuts I needed. Because those experts at whom I rolled my eyes were right: I'm still an alcoholic, I always will be and, despite however long

I've been off my substance of choice, I'm only one split-second of stupidity or self-delusion within being right back there. And I still don't feel particularly wise or transformed, like they promised. I never have. I just try to keep my head down, keep busy, and hope things keep moving forward.

This particular wagon tumble started - though it was probably building for months - it was one moment of panic about two hours before my daughter's guests arrived.

It was the White Claw that launched days of on-again, off-again episodes of deception, hiding, misplaced anger, uncomfortable admissions, emotionally-humiliating text messages disguised at bold-faced poetry, a half-assed attempt at contacting someone against whom I apparently still carry a grudge, a few days of hungover but acceptable work, and 36 hours of physical detox pain after deciding not to destroy everything I've built the past four years.

The White Claw was just the first stone in the avalanche.

Fire departments sometimes invite reporters out to a location somewhere with a lot of overgrown weeds just as fire season starts, to show how drought-starved California vegetation easily catches fire and takes off at a sprint. The TV people are the first to show up with cameras to set up for the best shots because fire looks great on TV. We bring photographers because, even in a controlled situation, people love fire photos.

My first year in journalism school, I had an awful teacher who liked to scare students. My reporting class at San Francisco State in

1995 started off with 24 students and ended the semester with four or five. He made one girl cry. He said he was doing us a favor by weeding out the weak and if we couldn't handle him, we couldn't handle a city editor at any decent sized newspaper. Which was absolute bullshit, of course. But he did say one thing that made a lot of sense, pointing out the difference between print journalism in 1995 and TV journalism. Find a fire story on either. Then see how the other guys covered it. Chances are the TV news led with the fire if they had film because fires are spectacular visuals. Meanwhile, unless there was a photo of a firefighter saving a baby in one hand and a puppy in the other, the fire story was probably relegated to page A12 of the newspaper. Because we on the print side were real journalists: malnourished, pale and unshowered, while the TV people wore makeup and pretended to like each other.

Actually, that's not totally true. I know some TV reporters who are much better journalists than me. But that used to be the well-worn cliche. I think the Internet has forced TV reporters to up their game.

Fast forward nearly 30 years to the era of climate change happening before our eyes and everybody leads with fire stories. So everyone now has lots of visuals of fires starting and taking off at 200 mph like the first row at the Indy 500. It's stunning how fast modern fires move these days.

Now, not to be overly dramatic … but that's exactly how I feel when I've started drinking again these past six or seven years. I think I'll be able to control the small burn at first (just like back in the good old '90s when I also got away with wearing construction boots with shorts). Then the wind picks up and the flame turns to an inferno, roaring like a Boeing 747 taking off over my head. Which, of course, is suddenly nearly impossible to stop.

This last one was a close one, though. I wasn't drinking while I worked, as if that gave my week some validity. I kept it to nights and the weekend because I knew I couldn't screw up another job, which I actually liked for the first time in years.

That White Claw wasn't my first drink of the weekend. It was just the sign that this was no isolated incident. The first drink happened the night before, just before my daughter's guests started arriving. She wanted to show off our new home to six or eight of her closest friends.

For three years we lived in an apartment that was about the size of a living room couch cushion fort connected to a card table with an old blanket thrown over the top. I dated someone for three months and refused to take her there because I was embarrassed about living so small. Which was stupid. We didn't host social gatherings. My mom came over once - and just once - probably to remind me how "cute" is a widely-used euphemism for "tiny." It didn't matter. We weren't having parties - we couldn't fit enough chairs for the four people we could fit inside - but that apartment represented a lot to me in retrospect. Mostly, that I could sober up and take back some control of my life.

It was kind of a dump. But it was our dump.

So when we stole my youngest girl back from my ex-wife

(we didn't steal her, be quiet) I went out on a limb. I rearranged my life (I'm not the best at change sometimes) and committed myself financially, not actually knowing whether I could make the numbers work every month. Screw it. We now live in a pretty big two-story house where it took me three months to discover we had a family room *and* a living room.

My daughter was ordering me around all week before the big party, which was fine. I let her have her fun. Then, right before her guests showed up, I realized "Good God, this is the first party at my house in seven years." I already spent too much time alone in my room and started feeling weird and claustrophobic. I didn't know if I could deal with a bunch of people drinking in my house. I started panicking that I had nowhere else to go and couldn't kick them out once they showed up. This from a guy who's never seen Canada but nevertheless once used Boxing Day as an excuse to throw a party.

So I went downstairs and grabbed a drink. My decision. My responsibility. And immediately felt better.

But not for long.

A week after the launch of the White Claw, after two pretty bad days of secret detox, secluded in my home with no lights and two days of Netflix, I emerged, remembered I had to work, and thought it was time to reawaken my body.

So I grunted my way down to the floor - slowly. Started to stretch my legs in what the P.E. teachers used to call a hurdler's stretch, which was me basically sitting up with my legs in a position a nine-month pregnant woman wouldn't have found challenging. It hurt … but it stretched. Nothing popped or burned - so far, so good.

Then I saw it … on my sock there was a piece of some sort of meat. A small piece. Probably barely chewable, I thought. Pinkish … maybe ham. Dried pepperoni. Canadian bacon … do they even have Canadian bacon anymore?

To my credit … I didn't eat it. Which may not have been the case a couple days earlier. It was gross, just like my old life. But it was small - a tiny reminder. I threw it away.

I laughed. It was absurd. I got off my ass, drank about a gallon of water, and got back to work. My daughter has since had another birthday; My youngest and I found somewhere else to sleep that night.

Chapter 12

Never Say Never, But ... Never

This is where I wrap things up and deliver a summation and/or lesson convincing children everywhere not to drink themselves into the dark, vomit-smelling abyss, from which it's very difficult to crawl out.

So just say no to the drunken abyss, kids. I'll tell you in person once I become a famous anti-alcohol advocate and visit your school, which will hold a special assembly in the gym, just for me to scare you.

Back in 1984, Nancy Reagan had every adult in America thinking they were bad parents for not stopping their teens from nose-sucking as much cocaine as they ... OK, we ... could jam into our faces. They couldn't have stopped us if they locked up our nostrils.

My school - California High School in the Bay Area suburb of San Ramon - treated us to a very special speaker for a very special assembly one day in 1984.

Some kids were still being forced to watch the 1978 documentary "Scared Straight," in which a group of convicts gets turned loose on some juvenile delinquents to scream at and intimidate them like mice thrown in a tank with a hungry python. That was the adult vibe coming at us. Don't do this or you go to prison to become someone's prom date every night. And, of course, while the Reagans were secretly selling deadly weapons to Middle Eastern enemies to kill South American commies, they were publicly scolding addicts to just stop doing those darned drugs. Stop shaking and throwing up and being homeless and lazy and just get a job and buy a house and live the American dream, will you?

It was the very confusing war on drugs, which ended up being a miserable failure because, while we were being told drugs were so bad, we were having so much fun with them.

We really were. As an addict whose life was nearly destroyed by substance abuse, I can still say ... my God, we had fun in the '80s.

Alcohol was apparently a different story. While adults yelled at us not to do drugs, plenty of them - including my stepfather - were buying us booze and occasionally drinking with us and having arm wrestling competitions with our friends (well, at my house anyway). With a drink in one hand, he'd responsibly collect every-one's keys, drink some more, wrestle some arms, drink some more, then load eight or nine drunk kids in his van a couple hours later to drunk-drive them home.

Right. A mixed message, to be sure. No wonder our fashion sense was so horrible. We were very confused.

But there was no confusion around the mustached former cop, whose rapid fire monologue made it seem he was the one sniff-ing buckets of cocaine that day at Cal High. He was allegedly - if I remember correctly - a former New York vice cop who told us high-speed, horrifying tales of his days dealing with drug addicts on the mean streets of NYC. One of his stories involved showing up to a drug-related disturbance call, only to find the drug addicted mother had cooked her own child in the family oven.

True or not, it was terribly shocking to an assembly of kids for whom tragedy constituted waking up to a non-functioning curling iron or finding one's Def Leppard jersey accidentally shrunk in the laundry. The teenage California girls cried and the guys just walked away stunned that awful afternoon. Being cynical, invincible, and kind of insensitive, I probably shrugged and went looking for cocaine.

If you're getting the idea cocaine was a big deal in 1984, you would probably still be underestimating just how big a deal cocaine was in 1984.

But I'll be honest back here in 2025. For me, stopping drugs was no big deal. Most of us - except for a couple friends and two former bandmates no longer alive because they discovered meth and heroin - simply grew out of drugs like cocaine. I realize it was a different time and recreational cocaine is almost Halloween candy compared to the lethal capabilities of modern street drugs.

But alcohol has been a completely different, more legal and acceptable story - even if I knew more friends who drank themselves to death. Breaking up with alcohol absolutely sucks, but it's absolutely necessary once you become dependent. Especially if you still want to interact with other humans. From your perspective, it's not because it will kill you, because there are frequent days when you just no longer care. But you'll be gone and everyone around you will be left to clean up the emotional mess.

For the addict, not only will quitting be the most difficult thing you ever do, but if left unchecked long enough, the alcoholism will simply destroy - or permanently damage - nearly every relationship in your life.

Here's my scared straight, child-in-the-oven pitch, only a bit more realistic: Alcohol will rip most of your friends away from you for good. Head over heels in love? Sucks for both of you, because you'll lose that person, too. Even if you sober up. Because unlike alcoholics, most people will never forget the horrible things you did that made you a monster who loved alcohol more than them.

They talk about stages of grief and it took a long time for me to get to acceptance. I wouldn't even use the term "alcoholic" for years. It's a major touchstone for many alcoholics - actually calling themself an alcoholic. I still dislike it. It reminds me too much of the yelling when I was a kid. But it's what I am.

Now I'm at a point of acceptance, but mourning my past life is limited to mostly my former friends. Next to giving my kids mental scars, driving away the woman I loved (I still hope sometimes, but I think my last go-round probably drove her away for good), and aging my poor mother prematurely, losing most of the friends I had since high school has been the most painful thing about becoming alcohol-dependent.

Mentally painful, I mean. All the falling down hurt, too. I admit it's kind of cool to tell people I've torn my rotator cuff twice - makes me feel like a kick ass, big league athlete. First time was from the very manly and athletic activity of lifting my daughter in and out of her crib. When mentioning the second, much worse time, I usually leave out the part about getting out of rehab, moving to Vallejo about 30 yards from a liquor store (handy tip: always check your surroundings before moving to a new city fresh out of rehab) and drinking my meals for a few days until I could no longer control my legs and subsequently crashed into a glass and iron table, somehow tearing my rotator cuff.

A year later when I finally couldn't deal with the pain anymore, I went to a doctor, who saw the damage and immediately scheduled surgery. Then I fell off the wagon again and I guess I didn't show up for surgery. My shoulder works again, finally, but the lingering pain is another of seemingly thousands of reminders not to drink that day.

The latest reminder is a fresh facial scar from falling and grating my face against the stucco on the outside of my house during the last fiasco. I think I have a new scar on my back as well, but can't say for sure, as I can't actually see it. My daughter says there's one, but I no longer trust people who buy White Claw.

When you're in a group of friends - and I was lucky to have a couple distinct groups of friends, anywhere from three or four to eight or ten people since high school (some since middle school) - they become pretty important. They're the ones with whom you let your hair down (literally - it was the '80s).

They're the ones you tell secrets and stupid jokes and cry and rant to about your girlfriend cheating on you (unless she's cheating with one of them, in which case they find a way to leave the room).

You go on roadtrips, have all your signature "firsts" around them, make memories, and laugh like your face is exploding. There's been an ongoing amateur comedy competition going on since 1981 among my friends. It was like a celebrity roast, only none of us were famous and it went on for three decades or so. Until they stopped inviting me.

At the end of these relationships, when your mind is too soaked to think clearly and the jokes fall flat, you get desperate and start doing things you did at parties when you were 20. Except now you're 40 and everyone has wives and kids and no one is really laughing anymore.

Right. People grow up. But alcoholism doesn't recognize the change. There's still a time and place for some foolishness, but the limits and venue for it are understood. Except by the guy who drinks too much.

So you stop getting invited because it's uncomfortable. And because you are, for lack of better descriptions, an idiot.

I've occasionally dreamt about my friends, being in places we used to go and doing the things we used to do. Then I wake up and immediately realize it will never happen again. I may never see some of them again. It's hard to get out of bed some days; others I have to fight the urge to drink it all away, like I used to. The battle is constant. And that's solely on me. Which takes us back to the disease of choice idea.

Which is why I'm whining about it here. Not because I want anyone to feel sorry for me (well, maybe a little). I'm really trying to warn someone off. If you wonder if you have a problem, chances are you do, or you're mighty close. I started wondering in 1995 and it took more than two decades to even start getting right (don't make the mistake of thinking just showing up for rehab will do much). If you're anywhere near there, throw on the brakes, cut way back, get healthy, and find something to replace the poison. And see how you feel. If there's a big improvement, then consider changing how much you drink.

Or try AA. While I'm not the biggest fan, I admit AA was very helpful when transitioning from rehab to real life. I still occasionally go. I've just found other things work better for me. But it's been around for nearly a century for a reason.

Of course, that all sounds as simple as the very serious and scientific Nancy Reagan solemnly asserting "Just Say No." But I repeatedly chose to activate the alcoholic monster in me. And now I'm paying for it and mourning friendships and people I love like they're dead, because I killed those relationships. The former life of the party went and killed the party.

They still go on, occasionally - which is how it works with healthy adults. I sometimes hear about gatherings to which I'm not invited. The week after my most recent relapse, I saw a social media photo of seven or eight of my buddies, smiling, (balding), wearing suits, beers in hands. I knew the pose well because I used to be in it. The caption described something to the effect of "I've been with these guys for 40 years and we're still bleh bleh bleh drinking and insulting each other bleh bleh and I love these dudes bleh bleh."

I sulked a bit, then remembered I took myself out of my social circle. I did that to me and sometimes it's painful. Then I remember I'm an adult, life changes and, my God, who gets to have the same swath of friends most of their lives? I was very lucky and try to be grateful. I have amazing memories.

There's really no "I would do anything for you" friend. Nor should there be; you shouldn't put friends in that position.

Then again, I was ostracized by a group of people known for, among other things, relentless partying. I really earned it. I imagine drinking everything in sight, throwing food, and pretending to give other men blowjobs at Christmas parties in your 40s isn't funny anymore - especially to wives. But choosing between wives and drunken high school friends isn't a choice for most reasonable men by then.

It's not their fault. And they all didn't give up. But I get it. Most of them just don't know what to do with me. I don't really know what to do with me.

Of course, it's not like I'm burning up the phone lines calling them. I let the relationships die because I was either too busy drinking or feeling embarrassed. I've stayed in contact with some. When I had no money to pay rent at the second sober living house I was eventually kicked out of, my buddy Sal actually called some of the gang and pulled together a couple grand or so to get me another month with a roof over me (until I got myself kicked out, not for drinking this time, but for keeping some pills from my last stint at the hospital I didn't know were on the house's naughty list). I thanked my friends very sincerely in a group text and don't think I heard back from many. But the gesture was appreciated and always will be.

It's not just friends you risk, of course. My family has stuck with me. As I've said, I know I've taken years off my mother's life. She loved me and kept trying to save me when no one else could. At one point she was literally my only contact to my former world when I was sleeping in her car in various parking lots at night. Because this disease of choice, if it doesn't rob you of your life, it robs you of most of the people in it.

My two surviving bandmates from my L.A. band (the only real band I was in, no matter what we all used to tell ourselves) stuck around and we're still close. One is also in recovery and we lean on each other almost daily. And when that's not enough, we call the other guy who's still in L.A. in the music business, where there's a higher percentage of addicts than at most rehabs. So he gets it. Our other bandmate is no longer here; he died about a decade ago after years of substance abuse. It wasn't his official cause of death, but his chances of still being around would probably have been much higher if not for addiction. He was very talented and received offers from acts you've heard of to play with them. But the chemicals ended up making it impossible. We also recently lost another former bandmate, from an early version of that "real" band, to a heroin overdose. He fought it for years and cleaned himself up, but it was still waiting for him and, after more than 35 years of fighting, the addiction finally won.

I also have a close friend left from one of my rehab stints and a girl I briefly dated who is now a good friend who, turns out, also has some alcohol issues. We occasionally have our own mini AA meeting, where we don't have to listen to people pretend a toaster can be your higher power just before they start praising Jehovah. There's nothing worse than detoxing and wishing you were dead at an AA meeting at which a grown man is standing and pointing at you, saying you have to find God.

Shut up … I didn't lose him. Where did you leave him?

But I have to show up for some sort of meeting. Because, even if you lose your friends, are done with rehabs, and don't like AA … you better find some people on whom you can lean. Or you're dead. It's that simple.

The aftermath of rejecting help for decades is everywhere. A couple months before I got my briefs in a twist over a stupid Facebook photo, I saw on social media my old colleagues from the newspaper had a holiday party, which included the retired people and those that went to other jobs. My old department, which included 15 to 20 fun and talented people, now employs just a few, from what I understand. The career I mourne doesn't exist anymore anyway.

So of course I understood. But it still bugged me. Of course I didn't expect to be invited. But I worked with those folks for 17 of my 23 years at the newspaper. I certainly made my own bed the last couple years I was there, then set the bed on fire and pushed it around the newsroom, pants dropped and screaming obscenities. When I bothered to show up.

I missed assignments. I missed gatherings. After I left, I missed funerals and wakes of colleagues about whom I cared and admired.

I still miss some of these people and my old career. Though I now have one for which I'm very thankful. I also realize, even if I didn't nuke my career, the newspapers I knew no longer exist. I'm very thankful I got in on the last few years of traditional newspapers crafted in a traditional newsroom. There's no place like it on Earth.

When I did show up to work Christmas parties, I drank too much (shocking), was too loud, filled my mouth up with whipped cream straight from the dispenser and pretended I was rabid (which I still think was kind of funny), etc.

Even through all those years, I simply never considered I wouldn't be around anymore. Though I always did sort of feel like I was on the edge of the frame, which was deliberate. I've never been much of a joiner - only when it came to bands and some sports. And, of course, my friend groups, of which I was always very proud.

My years-long rollover crash has finally, mostly, ended with me upright. A cautionary tale? Perhaps, if you like. People don't like talking about why you're not one of them anymore, and they definitely don't like talking about addiction. So I suppose the only way I can read the room is by omission. Oh yes. Even in a large group of high school buddies with whom, for decades, you drank like the Deltas in *Animal House* and competed to see who could act the dumbest. They will still stop calling when your alcoholic behavior becomes too much.

I don't blame them one bit. Nor do I write this to worm my way back into the circle or cast guilt. People are people. They grow up, get married, have kids, have grandkids - which is where many of my friends are at now - and the friendships you swore would never end get pushed down the list. They got pushed down my list as well. But never all the way off.

But no functional person in their 50s wants to deal with a stupid drunk at a social gathering. We're not teens with volcanic hormones, accidentally drinking too much from our parents' liquor cabinets anymore.

The good news is, about a week after feeling sorry for myself over not getting an invite to a holiday party, I went to an awards dinner for the first time in more than a decade. I won two awards for my work the previous year. The competition only covered about half the journalists still working in the Bay Area, but I'll take them (and did).

I don't want alcohol to be my legacy. Even if I am writing this much about it.

Even better, I've spent nearly five years living in my own place, with my daughters. From the time I left my home and family in 2017 until I moved into an apartment in 2020, I "lived" in five private homes (two were sober living facilities), not including two live-in rehabs (one twice), the detox from hell for five days, eight to ten days in the hospital (not including at least four trips to the ER), a night in jail, and a few scattered weeks with nowhere to live but a car or a park bench.

Was there anything good about that, other than the inherent lesson of alcohol addiction?

Yes. Moving so much made me have to get rid of at least half of what I owned. I'm healthier. I'm closer to being clear-headed. I'm close to my daughters who, unfortunately, saw my decline in all its humiliating stages. Hopefully it's a cautionary tale for them. I've also (mostly) stopped embarrassing myself to focus on what's important (what's left). All the attention I craved is no longer a priority.

And I may live for a while ... I hope.

Acknowledgements

Thank you Melissa Butler Phillips, Renny Madlena, Dan Rosentrauch, Stacey Roth, Chuck Barney, Mr.Clifton, Richie Thomas Keller, Kristine Carlson, Rob Barrett, Krista Cain, Sal Gallgher, Phil Jauriqui, Charlotte and John, Glory Marshall, Ken Brooks, Kat Rowlands, Randy McMullen, and Ms. Molloy.

About the Author

Tony Hicks is a reporter for Bay City News in the San Francisco Bay Area, where he grew up. He spent 23 years as a columnist, music and film critic, and news writer for Bay Area News Group (East Bay Times, San Jose Mercury News and Oakland Tribune). He's won more than two dozen national, state and regional journalism awards, mostly for columns and criticism. He loves to criticize. He also loves his daughters, two of whom still live with him because he apologized. He also has written for Medical News Today, Healthline, Riff magazine, Diablo magazine, Common Sense Media, BAM magazine and a few others willing to pay. He's also a recovering alcoholic. Before journalism, he spent his mid-20s in Hollywood because he thought he could be a rock star. He was wrong. This is his first book. Follow his nonsense on Twitter (X … whatever) at (@TonyBaloney1967), Bluesky at @tonybaloney1967.bsky.social, Instagram at tdhicks99, or Substack at https://substack.com/@tonybaloney666.

Made in the USA
Las Vegas, NV
03 July 2025

24440172R00125